1599   Moved to Southwark n__ ___ ____ _____ _____ which he and his company had recently erected.

1602   Extensive purchases of property and land in Stratford.

1602–4 Lodged with Mountjoy, a Huguenot refugee and a maker of headdresses, in Cripplegate, London. Helped to arrange a marriage between Mary Mountjoy and Stephen Belott, her father's apprentice.

1603   His company became the King's Majesty's Players under royal patronage.

1607   His daughter Susanna married Dr John Hall.

1608   Birth of Shakespeare's grand-daughter Elizabeth Hall.

1610   Shakespeare possibly returned to live in Stratford.

1613   Purchase of the Gatehouse in Blackfriars. Burning of the Globe Theatre during the première of *Henry VIII*.

1616   Marriage of his daughter Judith to Thomas Quiney in Lent for which they were excommunicated.

25 March, 1616   Shakespeare altered the draft of his will presumably to give Judith more security in view of her husband's unreliability and his pre-marital misconduct with another woman. His will also revealed his strong attachment to his Stratford friends, and above all his desire to arrange for the establishment of his descendants.

23 April, 1616   Death of Shakespeare.

1623   Publication of the First Folio edition of Shakespeare's plays collected by his fellow actors Heminge and Condell to preserve 'the memory of so worthy a friend'.

THE PLAYERS' SHAKESPEARE

A MIDSUMMER NIGHT'S DREAM

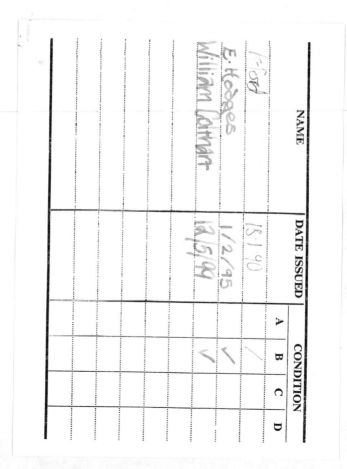

NAME	DATE ISSUED	CONDITION			
		A	B	C	D
P. Ford	15.1.90	/			
E. Hodges	1/2/95		✓		
William Latimer	13/5/94		✓		

A MIDSUMMER
NIGHT'S DREAM

Edited by

J. H. WALTER

M.A., PH.D.

Formerly Headmaster
Minchenden School, Southgate
Fellow of University
College, London

HEINEMANN EDUCATIONAL BOOKS

Heinemann Educational Books Ltd
Halley Court, Jordan Hill, Oxford OX2 8EJ

OXFORD   LONDON   EDINBURGH
MELBOURNE   SYDNEY   AUCKLAND
IBADAN   NAIROBI   GABORONE
KINGSTON   PORTSMOUTH NH (USA)
SINGAPORE   MADRID

ISBN 0 435 19005 9

Printed and bound in Great Britain by
Richard Clay Ltd, Bungay, Suffolk

CONTENTS

PREFACE

THE aim of this edition is to encourage pupils to study the play as a play, to see it not so much as a novel or a historical narrative, but as a pattern of speech and movement creating an artistic whole. While it has been generally accepted that this approach stimulates and enlivens classroom work, it has more recently become clear that it is a most fruitful way of preparing for examinations. The recent reports issued by the Cambridge Local Examinations Syndicate call attention to this aspect in the work of both Ordinary Level and Advanced Level candidates. The following comments are taken from the Advanced Level report:

'It will be seen that the best candidates are often those who show themselves conscious of the play as a made thing—usually, but by no means, always, as a thing made for the theatre' (p. 5). Again, 'And perhaps the most misunderstood aspect of Shakespeare is the part played by theatrical convention . . .' (p. 6).

The interleaved notes, therefore, contain, in addition to a gloss, interpretations of character, dialogue, and imagery, considered particularly from the point of view of a play. There are some suggestions for acting, for the most part simple pointers to avoid rigidity of interpretation and drawn up with an apron stage in mind. Some questions are interposed to provide topics for discussion or to assist in discrimination.

It is suggested that the play should be read through rapidly with as little comment as possible. On a second reading the notes should be used in detail, and appropriate sections of the Introduction might be read at the teacher's discretion.

It is hoped that this edition will enable the teacher to take his class more deeply into the play than the usual meagre allowance of time permits him to do; it is not an attempt to usurp his function.

The play was first published in quarto in 1600 and reprinted in 1619, and the First Folio 1623 used the quarto of 1619 as its copy. I have used a facsimile of the Folger Library copy of the quarto of 1600. I have also consulted the modern editions of C. J. Sisson, Sir Arthur Quiller-Couch and J. Dover Wilson, and the Furness Variorum edition. The text is complete. The locations of scenes added by previous editors have been placed in the notes. Reference to Shakespeare's plays not yet published in this series are to the Tudor Edition, ed. P. Alexander, 1951.

J. Dover Wilson's theory of textual revisions, put forward in the New Cambridge edition, 1924, and with added comment in his *Shakespeare's Happy Comedies*, 1962, is discussed in an appendix.

Among the many works from which I have gratefully drawn the following have helped me most: C. L. Barber, *Shakespeare's Festive Comedy*; K. Briggs, *Anatomy of Puck*; J. R. Brown, *Shakespeare and His Comedies*; G. Bush, *Classical Myth in Shakespeare's Plays*; Sir E. K. Chambers, *William Shakespeare*; G. K. Hunter, *John Lyly*; K. Muir, *Shakespeare's Sources*; R. Watkins, *Moonlight at the Globe*; J. Nichols, *Progresses of Queen Elizabeth*; E. Welsford, *The Court Masque*; E. C. Wilson, *England's Eliza*; J. Dover Wilson, *Shakespeare's Happy Comedies*; Alice Venezky, *Pageantry on Shakespeare's Stage*.

Similarly, I am indebted to articles by, among others, G. E. P. Arkwright, Dorothy Bartharum, N. Coghill, F. Kermode, M. Mincoff, and especially to a most stimulating article by P. A. Olson, '*A Midsummer Night's Dream* and the Meaning of Court Marriage'.

J.H.W.

INTRODUCTION

I

SOME nobleman's wedding celebrated between 1594 and 1596, and perhaps graced by the presence of Queen Elizabeth, seems to have inspired the wedding present of the writing and first performance of *A Midsummer Night's Dream*. Perhaps the banqueting hall or great chamber of a mansion was arranged after the manner of the entertainment reproduced on p. 19 for the players to 'beguile the lazy time' between 'after-supper and bed-time' on the bridal night. Two of the weddings, that have been suggested as possibly providing the occasion, demand consideration. One was that of the elderly Sir Thomas Heneage to the widowed Countess of Southampton on 2 May, 1594. A. L. Rowse has categorically claimed that the play was written for this and was performed in Southampton House. Possible topical allusions in the text, however, point to a later date. The other wedding was on 19 February, 1596 (sufficiently close in date to give point to the St. Valentine Day allusion in IV. i, 136–7) when Thomas Berkeley married Elizabeth Carey, daughter of Sir George Carey whose father was the Lord Chamberlain, patron of Shakespeare's Company. The wedding took place in Blackfriars close to the Blackfriars theatre used by the company. It would thus be easy and perfectly usual for the Lord Chamberlain to direct his 'servants' to provide a play for the celebrations. For the fairy parts they were no doubt assisted by singing-boys drawn from the musical establishment of the bride's father. It would be pleasant to speculate that Shakespeare, who had a hand in producing his plays, in convivial and festive spirit himself took the part of Quince.

J. Dover Wilson has argued strongly that the play was written about 1592, if not before, by someone other than Shakespeare, and that Shakespeare revised it on more than one occasion for presentation at several weddings between 1592 and 1598. The only certainties are that the play was performed in public by Shakespeare's Company before Francis Meres mentioned it in his *Palladis Tamia*, 1598, and that it was first published in quarto in 1600.

II

GENERAL COMMENTS

The varied nature of the play is reflected in critical comment. According to some it is mere gossamer and moonshine untouched by allegory; to others it is a symbolical, masque-like play containing not only moral allegory but traces of political allegory as well. To some it is courtly entertainment provided by a collection of parodies and burlesques on romantic love poems, amateur theatricals, classical legends, and platonic love; to others it is a serious comment on the nature of love, and an attempt 'to bring to life certain truths about wedlock'. To some it is 'barely more than a delicate, tenuous piece of decoration'; to others it has 'marked intellectual content'. Most agree, however, that its construction is ingenious and masterly in its reduction of incongruous elements to a harmony and rhythm that has prompted for it the analogy of a 'figured ballet'.

Apart from this agreement the comments appear contradictory and irreconcilable. It seems incredible that subtle care and delicate precision in craftsmanship on the one hand should exist alongside clumsy, botched, and immature workmanship on the other; or that serious intention in one place should be matched with aimless fairy-stuff or naive, artificial love-talk elsewhere. Here the view is taken that amid its frolic and farce the play is a careful, serious work of art as a whole, that its aim was, as in poetry, 'virtue-breeding delightfulness', or in Shakespeare's words on comedy, 'to hold, as 'twere the mirror up to nature; to show virtue her own feature, scorn her own image'.

The ritual and ceremony of the court naturally symbolic and

emblematic in its reverence for God's regent was exalted by the uniqueness of Elizabeth who as virgin, queen, and goddess was hailed as the thrice blessed. The devotion of her nobles and people was offered to her through personification, allegory, 'shadowed conceits' in the various modes of pastoral, chivalric, moral, and mythological entertainments, plays, poems, and pageants.

Entertainment at court, or for a special occasion either seasonal or personal in a nobleman's house or park, followed certain traditional patterns. Many of these had been gathered up in combination in the plays of John Lyly, and *A Midsummer Night's Dream* undoubtedly owes much to the example of his plays. Some of the ingredients such as the quarrel between Oberon and Titania, or the discovery of the sleeping lovers by the royal hunting party were the kind of shows that might have greeted Elizabeth while on a visit to one of her nobles. Others that occurred frequently in pageants, masques, shows, and in Lyly's plays, were classical legend and mythological characters (often taken from Ovid's stories), devices both serious and burlesque developed from the May King, Summer Queen, Lord of Misrule and other folk festivals, allegorical shows in the modified tradition of the Middle Ages, and the debating of topics. These aspects of the five plots in *A Midsummer Night's Dream*: the wedding of Theseus and Hippolyta, the lovers' entanglements, the dispute between Oberon and Titania, Titania's infatuation with Bottom, and the interlude of *Pyramus and Thisby*, are considered under separate headings below.

All these plots are concerned with love. They are not simple, but in their context of mythology, classical story folk-lore, and allegory have implicit significances. They are directed towards one end, Theseus' wedding, in which the mature, rational, and proper relationship between Theseus and Hippolyta also stands as the ideal pattern to which the lovers should aspire. They reveal, however, irrational attitudes and behaviour. Titania, a wayward wife, flouts the natural order, and her wilfulness projects her into the lowest form of infatuation. Lysander and Hermia, although aware of the transience and disorder of the love they call true, reject both the law and parental judgement and rashly elope; Helena doting 'in idolatry', pursues Demetrius and so reverses the natural order. Pyramus and Thisby also elope, but only to their death. In particular Shakespeare ridicules the 'heady force of frantic love' as a species of hallucination or illusion that may, as in *Romeo and Juliet*, lead to tragedy. Here the tragic implications of the lovers' flight to the wood are gathered up and purged away by the hilarious deaths of Pyramus and Thisby.

The movement of each plot is shaped by the balance of opposing ideas, and these paired ideas are facets of, or parallels to, such basic pairs as appearance and reality, or reason and imagination. Thus in the relationship and speeches of Theseus and Hippolyta the following opposites can be discerned:—male (reason)—female (fancy), reason—imagination, and justice—mercy. Theseus in fact frequently points out antitheses and submits them to his judgement: love—injuries, virginity—marriage, concord—discord, silence—eloquence. The lovers are concerned with truth and error, illusion and reality, dream and reality, transience and permanence. Hermia laments the unreality of true love; Helena proclaims that her heaven is now hell; and with nice irony Lysander in the frenzy of passion induced by the love-juice proclaims his arrival at a state of mature reason and judgement. Their misadventures take place in the haunted wood by night; their reconciliation appears before the orderly court in the rational light of day. Oberon holds the balance between chastity and desire, Bottom discourses on reason and love to Titania; he for the moment, although in beast shape and therefore devoid of reason, is ironically more rational than the amorous queen. The mechanicals are confused over reality and the illusion of the play, and this leads them to accept the delicious anomaly of casting Snout as a wall supported by the assurance 'I am that same wall; the truth is so'. Helena when wooed by both Lysander and Demetrius, erroneously concludes that they are acting a play at her expense. The climax of complexity between the stage illusion and reality comes in Act V. There, as Miss Bradbrook points out, 'in the mirror technique of the play within the play the fun puts both players and audience together inside the jest of professional actors pretending to be mechanicals trying to be amateur actors before an unreal audience'. One may perhaps wonder how far Oberon, the king of shadows, and his fairy court following darkness like a dream are airy nothings or have only a dream reality.

The changes of condition and the establishment of a dramatic situation are frequently brought about by the narration of past events. Theseus recalls his conquest of Hippolyta, and the stumbling speeches of welcome offered to him; Titania recalls Oberon's waywardness, the late disasters, and the birth of the changeling; Oberon recalls Titania's influence on Theseus and his version of Cupid; Helena speaks poignantly of her early friendship with Hermia; Hippolyta remembers her early days hunting in Crete. The emotional situation that calls them forth may vary, but in addition they give depth, spaciousness, and a timeless quality to the play.

Many writers have noticed the hints of evil and tragedy that occur. Evil things lurk in the wood. The fairies utter incantations to ward off witchcraft. Puck describes the ghosts and spirits that wander in the night, whereat Oberon declares, 'we are spirits of another sort'. Helena and Hermia fear the wild beasts of prey. Above all the wood is a place of fearful changes, of distorted vision, of illusion, even of dreams that threaten. This undertone of threat, fear, and death is a necessary part of the allegory of the lovers lost in the wood of error, and of the conflict between the forces of light and those of darkness.

III

THESEUS AND HIPPOLYTA

Among Shakespeare's comedies *A Midsummer Night's Dream* is

unique in having figures from classical mythology as important characters. This, however, is in keeping with the intention and occasion of the play. The value of such characters was their larger than human stature, their universality, their long-established emblem-like significance, and the familiarity of their idiom, particularly to sophisticated courtiers among whom emblems, symbols, and devices were commonplaces.

The wedding of Theseus and Hippolyta which Shakespeare has modified from his sources, is not only the frame and occasion of the events of the play, it also sets up an ideal pattern of love and marriage. Theseus had overcome the Amazons, the virgin warriors hostile to marriage, and in marrying their queen, Hippolyta, was assuming that dominance of husband over wife which was regarded as established by divine ordinance. It is described in the *Comedy of Errors*, II. 1, 20–4:

> Man, more divine (than beasts) . . .
> Indued with intellectual sense and souls . . .
> Are masters to their females, and their lords.

It is accepted by Portia who submits herself 'to be directed, As from her lord, her governor, her king'. Olson notes that the same view, stated specifically of Theseus and Hippolyta, occurs in the *Two Noble Kinsmen*, a play attributed to Fletcher and Shakespeare, I. i, 83–90. A queen addresses Hippolyta:

> wast near to make the male
> To thy sex captive, but that this thy lord,
> Born to uphold Creation in that honour
> First nature stilled it in, shrunk thee into
> The bound thou wast o'er-flowing.

This springs naturally from the terms of the legend, but the marriage relationship was supported by the belief that woman was an inferior creature of the senses and the passions, who therefore had to be restrained and directed by man who was endowed with a rational, intellectual soul. Here that 'monstrous regiment', the rule of women, has been overthrown by Theseus who has turned such conflict and disharmony into the right concord of peace and love, as he himself reminds the audience (I. i, 16–17).

The complete harmony and complementary natures of Theseus and Hippolyta are beautifully shown by the exquisite links of imagery, verbal device, and symbol in their opening speeches. Thereafter Theseus dominates their appearances. He expresses the rational view in his remarks to Hermia—the need to use judgement in love, to obey one's father, and the preference for marriage over sisterhood. Their arrival in the wood at dawn with a hunting party, apart from its dramatic convenience, is almost entirely symbolic. The order and harmony of the court now drive away the fears and errors of the forest 'night-rule', fled before the sweet thunder of the hounds. Theseus again imposes the superiority of his judgement and knowledge on Hippolyta. While waiting after supper he propounds a rational, sceptical explanation of the lovers' account of their adventures. When faced with a choice of entertainment his discrimination is coupled with magnanimity as he gives reasons for selecting *Pyramus and Thisby* and over-ruling Hippolyta's fears. Among his final remarks, 'Lovers to bed, 'tis almost fairy time' apart from its premonitory hint to the audience is surely a gentle touch of irony to the lovers recalling their account of the previous night's bedding.

Hippolyta's feminine nature is glanced at in her first speech with its stress on dreaming, in her pity lest the mechanicals' gallant attempt shall break down, and in her acceptance of a consistency in the lovers' stories albeit 'strange and admirable', and in spite of Theseus' rationalizing. For her

> Reason has moons, but moons not hers
> Lie mirror'd on her sea.

An interesting feature of Theseus and Hippolyta is their moving forward in time. They begin strictly in Athens but by Act V they have become an Elizabethan lord and his lady in their mansion.

IV

OBERON AND TITANIA

In the two of his comedies designed to celebrate a wedding Shakespeare introduces magic and fairies or spirits; in both they control and direct the action, either heal an ancient wrong or reconcile lovers, and bestow a benediction on marriage. Accordingly in *A Midsummer Night's Dream* Oberon and Titania are not mere whimsy to be regarded with amused condescension as pretty pieces of decoration, mere mouthpieces for topical allusions and courtly compliment, or devices to activate the machinery of the plot. To regard them as 'daintily ridiculous', and 'as a comically awful warning of what marriage may turn to if jealousy and temper get the upper hand' (Granville Barker) or as 'squabbling children' are patronizingly superficial judgements. Although Titania's relations with Bottom are comical in the extreme, they have allegorical significance, and likewise her relations with Oberon are intended to be seriously considered. Oberon should be allowed dignity and authority, otherwise the blessings he bestows on Theseus' marriage are empty words.

A widely differing view regards the relations of the two as a complete allegory following pageant practice and the plays of Lyly. In these higher love (Oberon) finally subdues rebellious earthly, sensual love (Titania) who had captured a rational soul (changeling) by reducing her love to the lowest physical infatuation for a beast (Bottom), and takes the rational soul into his (male) care. Again this goes too far in the direction of a morality play, but it does offer some explanation of things otherwise childish and naive. Yet another view connects them with the May games of the countryside, the observances in the woods in which the May King and the Summer Lady offer their wishes for joy and prosperity to their patron, the lord of the manor. Finally it has been suggested that some characteristics of Oberon and Titania show vestiges of a possible source in Pluto and Proserpine in Chaucer's *Merchant's Tale*.

Oberon and Titania, symbols of powers and passions, are descended from the gods of classical myth to become creatures of the moonlight and shadows, and lightly figured in human lineaments. Their quarrel, in which the 'rash wanton' Titania not only has 'forsworn' Oberon's 'bed and company', but also mocks his claim to be her lord, condemns her as a rebellious wife flouting the rightful dominance of her husband. By a neat transition in their tauntings—like characters in the entertainments presented before Queen Elizabeth—they announce that their presence is due to the love they bear the royal couple and their wish to offer blessings. At the same time their accusations reflect their symbolic nature. It was the influence of Titania (sensual love) that caused Theseus to love and leave so many women; it was Oberon (higher love) that attracted Hippolyta, or Pan-like that played to a shepherdess. They are also gods especially concerned with fruits, flocks, earth's increase, and the orderly progression of the seasons, all of which their discord has brought to destruction and chaos. Titania's concluding description of these disasters as a 'progeny of evils' to which they are parents is sharply ironic in that their progeny should be the fruitful increase of the earth. Her account of the birth and adoption of the changeling again marks her association with fertility, and her care for the rich merchandise, the fruit of love, and reveals her in the favourable light of former happiness.

Oberon, too, recalls a time of halcyon calm which by contrast with Titania's unrepentant departure signifies his association with the order and harmony accompanying the sea-maid's music. His vision, not vouchsafed to the humbler Puck, of the triumph of chastity over hot love has been taken as a metaphor of the whole play. It establishes Oberon's authority and power in the events that follow in the wood, and by its allusion to Queen Elizabeth enlarges him into the immediate present of the spectators. Armed with 'love-in-idleness' and 'Dian's bud' Oberon as a magician and invisible eavesdropper presides benevolently over the affairs of the lovers and less benevolently over his wife.

Titania's preparations for sleep carefully dissociate her and the fairies from any creature that has to do with witchcraft, a distinction that Puck and Oberon elaborate for themselves on a later occasion (III. ii, 381–8).

Her infatuation with Bottom portrays the degradation of physical love that lowers man to love a beast. Here, however, it gives no offence, it is pure comedy. The incongruity of beauty wooing the beast, Bottom's massive insensibility, the burlesque of the passionate declarations of the lovers, and of platonic love in the terms used by Titania normally to describe the communion of heavenly souls, must have provided mirthful fare for the courtiers.

Oberon is not wholly a king of shadows, he claims alliance with dawn and the rational light of day. He who brought about the changes and fantasies of the night links himself with the beneficent alchemy of daylight. His speech again balances the disorders narrated by Titania. His reunion with her after her submission to his will is celebrated with the harmony of music and dancing.

Music and dancing accompany their midnight incantations and blessings in Theseus' palace. Here perhaps they resemble the May King and the Summer Lady of Maying ceremonies, or the gods of pageant and entertainment, offering blessings and performing lustrations.

V

PUCK

Puck is a traditional figure from folk-lore. His native character is partly described by the Fairy, and Puck himself adds the further touches of his pranks as Oberon's jester. He is devoid of a sense of moral obligations, ironically mistaking the chaste separation

between Lysander and Hermia (II. ii, 76–7) as evidence of a
quarrel. In his activities as Oberon's messenger he plays a kind of
Cupid's role; he also acts as Oberon's herald and time-keeper.
The panic of the mechanicals, the preposterous situation of the
lovers, and the metamorphosis of Bottom afford him the greatest
delight. His final appearance with a broom 'To sweep the dust
Behind the door' not only recalls his benevolent activities, but for
the moment invests him with symbolic sweeping away of evil in
readiness for the lustrations and benedictions of Oberon and
Titania and their train.

VI

THE LOVERS

The lovers have been much abused. Egeus abuses Lysander,
Lysander abuses Demetrius, each abuses the other in the wood.
Puck condemns them as fools playing out a silly play. Editors and
commentators disparage their intelligence, their love-sentiments,
their behaviour, and the naive, mannered verse Shakespeare puts
in their mouths. Further, they are very slightly characterized, and
even that is usually by direct statement. Helena is tall and timid,
Hermia short, dark, and quick-tempered. Apart from Demetrius'
label of 'spotted and inconstant', and the accusations of cowardice
hurled at each other, there is not much to distinguish Lysander
from Demetrius. If Lysander is more eloquent earlier in the play,
Demetrius is the more liberal with his comments on the mechanicals' performance.

If they are regarded as attempts at realistic human portraits,
there is some justification for condemning them, but they are
surely shadows, dramatic pieces playing out a foolish pageant.
Puck's observation gives the correct interpretation, the folly of
infatuation and doting. Although their plot takes up more space
than that devoted to any of the other plots, it must not be regarded
as the main plot. It is subordinate to the wedding-theme of

Theseus and Hippolyta which it amplifies and ennobles by its contrasting love-sickness and absurdity.

The pattern of their actions—refusal to wed, elopement, complication, reconciliation—is common enough in comedies of intrigue, here it is given eccentric twists by the actions of Oberon and Puck. In the opening scene the conflicting situation is stated, and its implications soberly assessed by Theseus; in the wood the lovers play a frantic farce, which later they consider to be the illusion of a dream; finally they witness a burlesqued tragedy, a mocking imitation of their own actions, oblivious of the ironic similarities apparent to the audience.

All the lovers are confused and unreasoning. Lysander and Hermia, misunderstanding the nature of true love, flee from the judgement and order of parent and king; Demetrius is inconstant for no reason that Helena can discover. Helena, for whom life is so disordered that Demetrius' graces paradoxically have turned her paradise of love into the hell of rejection, in her unbalance betrays her friend Hermia to Demetrius. In the dark, enchanted wood all lose their way. The wood is a place of real peril; it is also the wood of error like that in the *Faerie Queene*, a symbol of the dark world of evils that beset the man who allows his senses to dominate him. The inflaming force of the love-juice deceives Lysander and Demetrius into proclaiming with irony that reason and maturity now govern their love. All grope hopelessly after truth. Helena assumes that Lysander, Demetrius, and Hermia are each playing a part to mock her. She too with irony in the light of her earlier breach of friendship, accuses Hermia of a similar breach. The more frantically earnest they protest, the more comically ludicrous they become. All four are in error which plunges them into strife, the accepted fate of those who succumb to the illusion of passion and desire. Hermia's attempt to fight Helena, a parody of the intended duel between the two men, is the final touch of comic absurdity.

Awaked into the rational daylight world of Theseus' court the events of the night seem to them as dreams. While Theseus utters astringent comments on their tales, Hippolyta's words perhaps hint at the parable of their story, 'all their minds transfigured so together . . . grows to something of great constancy.'

VII

THE MECHANICALS

The preparation and presentation of *Pyramus and Thisby* by the mechanicals has more than one intention. It reflects the disaster that may befall rash elopements but in an atmosphere of pantomime and farce, and it mocks the amateur play-productions of craftsmen from the guilds. It may perhaps parody the kind of play presented by the Children's Companies at court. Flute's remark that Bottom would have deserved sixpence a day may humorously hint at this, for sixpence was the daily allowance for each of the Children of the Chapel Royal—the Gentlemen of the Chapel were allowed the higher rate of sevenpence halfpenny.

The individual mechanicals are lightly differentiated with endearing human touches: Starveling shows signs of bad temper, Flute is becomingly modest about his beard, Snug has anxieties about learning his part, Snout has the rudiments of an inquiring mind. They are at one in their anxiety to avoid giving offence to their audience, particularly the ladies, and in their failure to understand dramatic illusion, they fear lest stage presentations should be mistaken for reality.

Quince, nervous and hesitant, is prompted by Bottom at their first appearance. It may be that his speech (I. ii, 4–6) has in it the seeds of uncertain order that blossomed later in his famous prologue. He solves in a knowledgeable way the simple difficulties raised by Snug and Flute. On occasion he can be firm and adroit in handling Bottom, either by playing off the fears of the duchess against the approval of the duke, or by flattery when it comes to casting Pyramus. Gaining confidence and authority he even cracks an ancient joke before announcing further plans. He produces prologues to order and suggests the personification of the moon, but perhaps out of weariness before the exuberant fancy of Bottom he accepts the latter's 'Some man or other must present Wall'. It is not so much that carpenter Quince and joiner Snug could easily have made a stage wall, but the reduction to the absurd of the device of using a man to personify some thing, in this case an impersonable object. In what should have been his moment of triumph, he stammers out the disastrous prologue, and thereafter he is busied with the affairs of prompter and producer.

Bottom steals the show. Whether he is a caricature of Robert Greene, another playwright or not cannot now be determined. There is more ground for thinking that Shakespeare played on the known characteristics of Kempe, the clown who presumably first played Bottom. Kempe, it has been suggested, was apt to interpolate matter of his own into his part, he was difficult to handle, and Bottom's desire to play all parts may be a hit at him. Similarly the quips on Bottom's voice—his roaring like a nightingale, his singing that entranced Titania, and Quince's praise, 'a very paramour for a sweet voice' may ironically point to a loud-mouthed Kempe.

In his own right Bottom is a leader, he overflows with suggestions, and his fellows respect him as 'sweet bully Bottom'. He is enthusiastic with a a child's facility for dropping one thing when another proves more attractive. He assumes responsibilities, praising a play he has not read, pointing out difficulties for which he provides solutions. Priestly and Coghill see Bottom as an artist. He cares for style, he is concerned about make-up, prefers the amplitude of 'eight and eight' as more appropriate to the subject than 'eight and six'. His confidence in himself and his desire to excel sometimes defeats his vocabulary.

Abandoned by his fellows in the wood, he is usually praised for his courage. On the contrary he may be horribly afraid. His little song, a kind of St. Valentine's Day posy, so unexpected from one who delighted in 'Ercles' vein', may signal his quavering fear. As a weaver he may have sung it to a psalm tune. Again, he is held to show poise and confidence in his encounter with Titania, but cannot the episode be played as if he is thoroughly nervous, edging away in alarm from amorous enticements like a puritanical weaver? Are his little jokes with Peaseblossom and the other fairies nervous, masterful or simpletonian? The tying up of Bottom's tongue is usually interpreted as a silencing of his loquacity, but silence was one of the conditions for entering fairyland; even Oberon and Titania travel in 'silence sad'. In Titania's bower he is king Bottom reigning with childish delight and completely insensible to Titania's blandishments. Passionate beauty pursuing the innocent simpleton who fails to see her advances is good farce. Bottom remains rational at a humble level, yet his requests not only ironically hint at his translated state, but they are an effective anti-climax to Titania's passion, and amusingly reflect the theme of reason against love.

Commentators have wandered in 'quaint mazes' over Bottom's soliloquy on his dream. One goes so far as to call it 'the supreme moment of the play . . . the awaking of the spiritual life in the animal man'. The echoes of 1 *Corinthians*, ii. 9–10, have been taken variously as innocent parody or of deep significance. The *Great Bible* version is suggestive:

'But as it is written. The eye hath not sene, and the eare hath not heard, nether have entred into the hert of man, the thynges which God hath prepared for them that love hym.

But God hath opened them unto us by his sprctc. For the sprete searcheth all thinges, ye the botome of Goddes secretes.'

And in verse 14: 'The naturall man perceaveth not the thinges that belonge to the sprete of God. For they are but folyshnes unto him.'

The whole passage describes the inability of man to understand spiritual things unless he is helped by the holy spirit. Was Shakespeare, who so delicately sits on the fence, mindful of the ass that saw the angel in the way when its master could not (*Numbers*, xxii. 23), or of the man transformed into an ass that saw the vision of the goddess Isis (*Golden Ass*)? Has he made Bottom's exaltation confuse his tongue over the senses which were confused elsewhere (III. i, 79; V. i, 190–1)? Is there a satirical glance at weavers, noted for their piety and psalm-singing, in that Bottom fails to quote the scriptures accurately? The scriptural allusion seems a deliberate and not a superficial jest. Perhaps the great innocent Bottom moved to ecstasy by his dream tries to quote the passage as the nearest phrases to describe his experience. The muddle is hilarious, but is there a touch of pathos?

Bottom returns elated, delighting in the mystery that surrounds him, infecting the others with his energy and excitement. In the interlude he is in his element. Conscious of his audience, indeed their comments destroy the dramatic illusion, he is prompt to step out of his part to patronize and correct Theseus. Perhaps he got his sixpence a day pension.

VIII

ELIZABETHAN STAGE PRACTICE AND THE PLAY

The stage conditions described in Appendix 3 determined to a large extent the shape of the plays, their dramatic devices, their methods and conventions.

The limited scenery gave the dramatist freedom to shift the scene of his play as often as he liked (*Antony and Cleopatra* has thirteen scenes in Act III). *A Midsummer Night's Dream* is conveniently arranged for some scenery changes. If it was originally performed in the hall of a house, some setting for the forest scenes may have been devized: the flowery bank and Titania's bower. The final performance of *Pyramus and Thisby* could then have been presented very much in the manner of the painting produced on p. 19. Shakespeare may change the scene unannounced

National Portrait Gallery

A MASQUE, POSSIBLY OF THE FAIRY QUEEN
AND ATTENDANTS, AT SIR HENRY UNTON'S
MANSION, *c.* 1595.

while the actors remained on the stage (*Twelfth Night*, III. iv, begins in Olivia's orchard and ends in the street), or, where knowledge of locality was not necessary for the understanding of the plot, he places it nowhere in particular, or in a place inconsistent with an earlier statement (*Julius Cæsar*, IV. i). Quarto and Folio acts and scenes are not normally introduced with any statement of where they take place. The precise locating of every scene would distract attention from the plot; the scene is where the actors are. Such imprecision coupled with the uninterrupted flow of the play helped to maintain the dramatic spell.

Shakespeare treated time with freedom. Inevitably some scenes overlapped, but he placed scenes out of their chronological order, he foreshortened time, or sometimes he merely confused it. What happens to the four days between I. i and V. i? When did Oberon meet Titania 'of late behind the wood' (IV. i, 45), and Philostrate witness a rehearsal of *Pyramus and Thisby* so that Bottom could announce 'our play is preferred' (IV. ii, 33)? His concern is not with the orderly sequence of events in real life but with the illusion of time in a play.

Most of the play takes place at night. Is there any ground for thinking that this true of I. i and ii? It fits, however, with the suggestion that the play, like the interlude, was intended to 'wear away this long age of three hours Between our after-supper and bed-time' at a private performance. The frequent references to night, directly or indirectly in the text, in Acts II, III and IV. i, 1–99 keep the situation clear in the minds of the audience who otherwise would have assumed that the action was taking place by daylight.

An important convention was the use of the soliloquy and the aside. The jutting out of the stage into the middle of the theatre floor brought the actors who were well forward nearer to the bulk of the audience than to actors at the rear of the stage. It had long been established that character and motives were announced directly, the audience was not left to guess what was going on in a character's mind. It was a simple matter, therefore, for an actor to come forward out of earshot of the others on the stage and reveal confidentially to the audience his character, his motives, and his intentions. In this way Shylock and Richard III declare their villainy, Prince Hal his intention to give up his bad companions, and Olivia her love for Viola. This device linked actor and audience intimately: the spectators shared in the play, they had a god-like knowledge of the hearts of the characters, and the two things were used to increase their feelings of tension and suspense, and the moments of dramatic irony. The aside, a brief pointed remark, is often ironic, or it may give the audience a kind of nudge to remind them of some matter. It too sustains the sense of intimacy between actor and audience.

A Midsummer Night's Dream, makes no use of the aside at all. Further the soliloquies of Helena I. i, 226–51; II. ii, 88–99, and Hermia II. ii, 145–56 are not revelations of character, they are straightforward expressions of emotion and statements of intended action. In other words the plots have a narrative shape, each one unfolds simply without complexity in its own frame.

There is some eavesdropping by Oberon in II. i; III. ii and by Puck in III. i and III. ii, Oberon perhaps wearing a cloak of invisibility (II. i, 186) (See Appendix, p. 181). This over-looking with the possibility of intervention, particularly by Puck, lends a touch of piquancy to these episodes.

The presence of characters asleep on the stage when other characters are in action increases tension and suspense. Titania with the love juice on her eyes sleeps while first Lysander and Hermia then Demetrius and Helena, and then the mechanicals appear. Excitement is raised in the expectancy that Titania will awake on each fresh arrival. It would have been in keeping with romantic plot had she awakened to fall in love with Lysander or Demetrius, but Shakespeare, after twice rousing the audience's anticipation, springs an unexpected and incongruous surprise in Titania's waking and immediate love talk to Bottom.

The ornate stage, the magnificent costumes, the royal and noble characters produced an element of formal pageantry in the performance of the plays. Gesture and stage business were formal dignified and restricted (except for the activities of a Puck) and the emphasis was placed on the delivery of speeches. To an audience accustomed to the impressive oratory of preachers at St. Paul's Cross, to sustained and eloquent speaking by its notabilities trained in rhetoric, the words of a play were particularly important. A well-spoken passage of rich word-painting reporting, for example, some event that had happened off stage was rousing and satisfying. It was a kind of pageantry in speech, or as a Jacobean writer put it, 'an ampullous and scenicale pomp' of words.

IX

VERSE AND PROSE

The impact of dialogue was enhanced by its traditional verse form; it gave to the major characters an impressive grandeur, a stature larger than life. In Shakespeare's plays its range, power, and flexibility are truly astounding, and he contrasts it from time to time with passages of prose almost as varied in style and form.

Shakespeare's verse is infinitely varied. At one extreme he may use heroic couplets to form a stately, stylized narrative in *Richard II*, at the other two speakers may express the perversity of things in couplets divided between them, the second speaker commenting on a statement by the first speaker as in I. i, 194–201. A few couplets appearing in the midst of blank verse passages may mark a heightening of emotion; a single couplet may mark a wise or significant saying, or an important exit. Frequently they impart a sense of finality, of steps taken from which there can be no turning back. There is plenty of evidence in Shakespeare's comedies and elsewhere that rhyme (often couplets) is the proper vehicle for expressing love. As rhymes can also express scorn and derision (*Cymbeline*, V. iii, 55) some love rhymes are held in contempt as mere balladry. In *A Midsummer Night's Dream* the changes from blank verse to rhyme and vice versa are skilful and significant. It is worth considering whether the lovers' rhymes are tinged with derision or not.

In early plays such as *Love's Labour's Lost* and *Romeo and Juliet* Shakespeare used both couplets and elaborate rhyme patterns. The first words Romeo and Juliet speak to each other taken together form a sonnet. Such patterns employed with elaborate figures of speech are by contrast with what has just been said a sign of the depth, strength, and sincerity of the speakers' feelings and are particularly employed in love scenes.

Shakespeare's blank verse too can be elaborate, enriched with swiftly following metaphors, with similes and other figures of speech or tricks of style, and with mythological allusions; it can be plain and direct; or it can become exaggerated and violent in language in the description of warfare, in frenzied appeals to the heavens, and in boasting. Its rhythms can march with regular beat, or, particularly in later plays like *King Lear* and *Antony and Cleopatra*, the rhythms are infinitely varied to achieve the most subtle effects. The characters use the kind of blank verse appropriate to the dramatic moment and not necessarily the kind consistent with what is known of them elsewhere in the play.

A Midsummer Night's Dream contains blank verse, lengthy passages in heroic couplets together with a few other rhyming patterns, and a number of short line couplets. Some editors consider that the variations are due to revisions of the play on two occasions, and that the heroic couplets were written about 1592, while some of the blank verse by its maturity of style was composed about 1598. There may have been alterations to the original play, but considerations of style are not by themselves very reliable, especially if alternative explanations of the variations are available. It is suggested here that the variations reflect clearly enough the estate of the speakers, their significance, their mood, or the content of their dialogue.

Blank verse is the staple medium of expression of the court. Theseus, Hippolyta and their courtiers speak it except during the presentation of *Pyramus and Thisby*, where their comments in prose contrast with the stiff rhyming of the interlude. Theseus' verse is dignified, smooth, always well-controlled, and furnished with apt illustrations to support his exposition of marriage and sisterhood or the vagaries of the imagination.

Yet blank verse can also express disharmony of character or incident when it intrudes on regular couplets used as a medium for expressing the harmony of love. Oberon and Titania quarrel in blank verse, and likewise Oberon describes to Puck the ending of the quarrel. Elsewhere Oberon speaks in couplets, and there he is concerned with the love juice, the various love affairs and his final ordering of matters as dawn breaks. Titania, perhaps as a rebellious wife, is to be regarded as the cause of discord for she normally speaks in blank verse except when she woos Bottom, III. i, 136 ff. (perhaps the incongruity of embracing Bottom reduces her to blank verse, in IV. i, 37–42!), and in her new found love for Oberon joins him in rhyme, IV. i, 73–99.

Lysander and Hermia speak blank verse at court and in the disorder of their minds following Theseus' judgement on Hermia; but in the uprush of emotion when Lysander proposes elopement, Hermia breaks into couplets, I. i, 171–8, and this medium continues in the love discussion which follows with Helena. Demetrius, a discordant figure, harshly rejects Helena in blank verse though he is moved to plead with Hermia in rhyme. The complete breakdown of love-relationships among the lovers is marked by a change from couplets to blank verse when Helena starts to reproach Hermia, III. ii, 195. When, however, the quarrelling lovers are spell-drawn by Puck they speak again in couplets. The precise relationships of verse forms to subject matter does not suggest that the variations are due to revisions.

Occasionally four lines have alternate rhymes perhaps as complete speeches to set themes at the beginning of fresh episodes, II.

ii, 35–8; IV. i, 1–4. Again, such four lines may have a couplet added to them to form a closing cadence to an episode, III. i, 95–100, 177–81 (five lines); III, ii, 431–6, 442–7, or to advance and clinch an argument, III. ii, 122–7, 128–33. In both their function resembles that of the sestet of a Shakespearian sonnet.

The short-lined couplets, here as in *Macbeth*, are used for spells and incantations; in addition they shape a fairy song and blessing, V. i, 387–406, or fairy talk, IV. i, 90–9; II. i, 2–13, or Puck's epilogue.

Prose is normally used by comic or low characters as befitting their rank, and by contrast with the verse spoken by the courtiers. It can present the stumbling conversation of a Dogberry or Verges, the chop-logic of Feste and Touchstone, the wit and expressiveness of Benedick and Beatrice, the passion of Shylock, and the pensive mood of Hamlet. Shakespeare's concern was always with dramatic effect. After Cæsar's murder, Shakespeare made Brutus, who elsewhere spoke blank verse, utter a flat, uninspired speech to the mob as a sharp contrast to the full power of the blank verse speech he gave Antony.

In *A Midsummer Night's Dream* the prose used by the mechanicals is colloquial and flexible, garnished with an occasional malapropism or oddity of phrasing, or with an oratorical flight by Bottom amid his short, direct sentences. In Act V the court party make their sharp comments on *Pyramus and Thisby* and its players in prose, an effective contrast to the couplets of that play, and the short rhymed verse of the passioning of Thisby and Pyramus.

X

IMAGERY AND VOCABULARY

The play has no profound soul-searching, the emotions of its characters are very much on the surface; accordingly its imagery has not the energy and fiery fusing of the images in the great tragedies. Simple similes are frequent: the moon is like a step-dame, or a 'silver bow Newbent in heaven', love is 'Brief as the lightning in the collied night'. Many of the metaphors are directly stated: 'Your eyes are lode-stars', 'The cowslips tall her pensioners be'. Long sustained images are rare though one occurs at II. i, 112–17: 'childing'—'increase'—'progeny'—'parents'—'original'. It has been noted that some of the flower metaphors are anthropomorphic: 'earthlier happy is the rose distilled' (I. i, 76), 'The cowslips tall her pensioners be' (II. i, 10) 'the green corn . . . beard' (II. i, 94–5). This infusion of personification, particularly in the speeches of the fairies, adds depth and suggestiveness to descriptive passages.

Certain words, or ideas associated with them, occur frequently: moon, moonlight, moonshine, starlight, night, darkness, shadows, dreams, flowers and fruit, creatures, eyes, sight, changes of state, music, dance, song, love, reason, imagination. They illustrate effectively the general atmosphere of the play and some of its thematic designs.

The speech of the mechanicals is sprinkled with such malapropisms as 'defect' (III. i, 34), 'disfigure' (III. i, 52), 'odious' (III. i, 70), 'exposition' (IV. i, 35), 'deflowered' (V. i, 283) which not only caricature them but also prevent the audience from accepting with seriousness their earnest endeavours.

XI

PUNS

An effort of imagination is required if we are to appreciate the importance and value of the puns that Shakespeare uses so frequently. What has been regarded in recent times as the lowest form of wit, was, as Kellett has shown, used with telling force by Isaiah and St. Paul and by the Greek dramatists. Among the Elizabethans it was an accepted means of showing intellectual brilliance and verbal dexterity. Shakespeare enlarges its scope; it may produce a simple jest or emphasize a point (Lady Macbeth's

> I'll gild the faces of the grooms withall
> For it must seem their guilt

is horrifyingly emphatic, it is not hysterical).

It may sharpen the irony of an aside ('A little more than kin and less than kind'); it may be a flash of bitter insight (in *Romeo and Juliet*, the gay Mercutio mortally wounded says, 'Ask for me tomorrow, and you shall find me a grave man'); and it may be employed in an exchange of witticisms.

Sometimes Shakespeare used the two meanings of a word simultaneously, sometimes the word is repeated bearing a second meaning, or sometimes a word may have the meaning of a word of similar sound imposed upon it (in *Love's Labour's Lost* 'haud credo' is confused with 'ow'd grey doe', and in *As You Like It* 'goats with Goths').

In *A Midsummer Night's Dream*, apart from Quince's ancient jest about 'French crowns' and playing 'barefaced' (I. ii, 81–2), a crack that adds the human touch to the figures of the mechanicals, and Bottom's play on 'sweet breath' (IV. ii, 36), the puns spring from the lovers and Theseus. It is significant that Oberon, Titania, Puck and Hippolyta do not pun.

Outbursts of emotion are intensified by puns. Demetrius savagely shouts that he is 'wood within this wood' (II. i, 192); Helena mourns the melting of Demetrius' 'hail' of oaths (I. i, 243–5). Hermia alone of the lovers does not pun, although she takes up an image from Lysander and extends it (I. i, 130–1). Lysander 'riddles very prettily' indeed. His impassioned plea for bed-room beside Hermia framed within the play on 'sense' and 'innocence' and the conclusion 'lying so, Hermia, I do not lie' (II. ii, 45–52) is delicately and graciously countered by her sincerity and tact. In V. i the punning and quibbling comes from Theseus, Lysander, and Demetrius, Helena and Hermia are silent throughout. It is mere wit-craft, mere word-play uninformed by emotion. Considered by itself the performance of *Pyramus and Thisby* would be too unintelligent and palpable-gross unless seasoned by the teasing and jests of the stage spectators. Its descant of raillery controls the attitude of the real audience, confirms the restored normality and wits of the courtiers, Lysander and Demetrius, and perhaps it helps to establish Theseus' magnanimity and graciousness in praising the players at the end.

A MIDSUMMER NIGHT'S DREAM

CHARACTERS

THESEUS, Duke of Athens
EGEUS, father to Hermia
LYSANDER ⎱ in love with Hermia
DEMETRIUS ⎰
PHILOSTRATE, Master of the Revels to Theseus
PETER QUINCE, a carpenter
SNUG, a joiner
NICK BOTTOM, a weaver
FRANCIS FLUTE, a bellows-mender
TOM SNOUT, a tinker
ROBIN STARVELING, a tailor
HIPPOLYTA, Queen of the Amazons, betrothed to Theseus
HERMIA, daughter to Egeus, in love with Lysander
HELENA, in love with Demetrius
OBERON, King of the fairies
TITANIA, Queen of the fairies
PUCK, or Robin Goodfellow
PEASEBLOSSOM ⎫
COBWEB ⎪ fairies
MOTH ⎬
MUSTARDSEED ⎭

Other fairies attending their King and Queen. Attendants on
Theseus and Hippolyta

SCENE: *Athens, and a wood near it*

Athens. The Palace of Theseus

A full ceremonial entry, perhaps heralded by fanfares, to a throne-hall. Should Theseus and Hippolyta enter separately and meet, or enter together? Is it night time or day time?

S.D.   *Theseus*, a legendary hero of Greece, the son of king Egeus. After slaying the minotaur and succeeding his father he made war against the Amazons, a tribe of women warriors. He defeated them and married their queen, Hippolyta.

       Why should Shakespeare have chosen the wedding of Theseus and Hippolyta from classical story as his framework for the play— to avoid giving offence to the unmarried reigning queen, to appeal to courtiers among whom classical allusions were fashionable, to display reason (Theseus) in control of the senses (Hippolyta), to show the natural relation of man holding domination over woman hitherto uncontrolled?

3–6   *But . . . revenue.* Does this sudden change from 'apace' show impatience, irritation, grief, playfulness, amusement, flattery of Hippolyta?

4   *wanes.* To marry during a waning moon was thought to bring misfortunes, so that weddings were solemnized during the time of the new moon. *lingers*, delays the fulfilment of.

5   *step-dame*, i.e. a second wife and likely to be young at the time of her husband's death. *dowager*, a widow to whom money is paid out of her husband's estate which after her death will pass to the heir.

6   *withering*, (*a*) wasting away, (*b*) as 'th' was sometimes pronounced 'd' there may be a glance at 'widow'.

7   *steep*, (*a*) be absorbed in, (*b*) sink in. See Sonnet 63, 'age's steepy night'.

9–10   *moon . . . heaven.* An apt simile for Hippolyta, the Amazon, whose symbol was the crescent moon.

       The speeches of Theseus and Hippolyta are finely complementary in thought, image, and construction. The imagery also sets the mode of the play.

13   *pert*, sprightly. *nimble*, lively, brisk.

15   *pale companion.* See *Pericles*, I. ii, 2, 'The sad companion, dull-eyed melancholy'. *companion*, fellow (contemptuous).

ACT ONE

SCENE ONE

Enter THESEUS, HIPPOLYTA, PHILOSTRATE, *and* ATTENDANTS

THESEUS: Now, fair Hippolyta, our nuptial hour
  Draws on apace. Four happy days bring in
  Another moon. But, o, methinks, how slow
  This old moon wanes, she lingers my desires,
  Like to a step-dame or a dowager,
  Long withering out a young man's revenue.
HIPPOLYTA: Four days will quickly steep themselves in night,
  Four nights will quickly dream away the time;
  And then the moon, like to a silver bow
  New-bent in heaven, shall behold the night   10
  Of our solemnities.
THESEUS: Go Philostrate,
  Stir up the Athenian youth to merriments,
  Awake the pert and nimble spirit of mirth,
  Turn melancholy forth to funerals;
  The pale companion is not for our pomp.   [*Exit Philostrate*

16–17   *I . . . injuries.* It was believed that men were by divine order the dominant sex. Theseus by defeating Hippolyta had restored the natural order of the universe. The point is made clear in the *Two Noble Kinsmen*, a play attributed in part to Shakespeare, where the Second Queen addresses Hippolyta, 'thy arm . . . wast near to make the male / To thy sex captive, but that this thy Lord, / Born to uphold creation in that honour / First nature 'stilled it in, shrunk thee into / The bound thou wast ore-flowing, at once subduing / Thy force and thy affection.'

19   *triumph,* formal procession and pageants.

S.D.   Is Egeus' entry—agitated, fussy, obsequious, pompous, ridiculous, dignified, enraged?

     Is he dragging Hermia in, beckoning her to follow, or is she following with Lysander? Is there any sign of enmity between Lysander and Demetrius?

20   *duke,* prince. Chaucer's word.

21   *Thanks . . . thee.* Is Theseus surprised, irritated at the intrusion, unruffled?

22–45   *Full . . . case.* Is Egeus' speech rapid, stuttering, high-pitched, slow, ponderous, snarling, quavering, grating?

27   *bewitched . . . child,* charmed away her heart, fascinated her heart. *bewitched.* Some editors change to 'witched'. Sisson omits 'man'.

28   *Thou, thou.* Egeus chokes with wrath. *rhymes,* posies, perhaps inscribed on the love-tokens. Scornfully emphatic.

31   *feigning,* (a) pretending deep feelings, false, deceitful, (b) yearning. The repetition and quibble point the sarcasm.

32   *stolen . . . fantasy,* caught her impressionable fancy.

33   *gauds,* toys, finery. *conceits,* fancy things.

34   *Knacks,* ornaments, trinkets.

     What is the effect of this on Hermia and Lysander? Does Egeus gesture or move in any way?

41   *privilege,* right.

44   *law.* Perhaps Shakespeare recalled Solon (d. 558 B.C.) celebrated for his law-giving and wisdom.

45   *Immediately,* directly, expressly. *case,* (a) event, (b) case (law), cause.

46   *Be advised,* think over carefully, consider deeply.

47–50   *To . . . imprinted.* Theseus picks up the metaphor from 'impression', l. 32. He stresses that Egeus as Hermia's creator should have the creator's right to do as he pleases with his creation.

Hippolyta, I wooed thee with my sword,
And won thy love, doing thee injuries.
But I will wed thee in another key,
With pomp, with triumph, and with revelling.

Enter EGEUS, HERMIA, LYSANDER, *and* DEMETRIUS

EGEUS: Happy be Theseus, our renowned duke.   20
THESEUS: Thanks good Egeus. What's the news with thee?
EGEUS: Full of vexation come I, with complaint
  Against my child, my daughter Hermia.
  Stand forth, Demetrius. My noble lord,
  This man hath my consent to marry her.
  Stand forth, Lysander. And my gracious duke,
  This man hath bewitched the bosom of my child.
  Thou, thou, Lysander, thou hast given her rhymes,
  And interchanged love-tokens with my child.
  Thou hast by moonlight at her window sung,   30
  With feigning voice, verses of feigning love,
  And stolen the impression of her fantasy
  With bracelets of thy hair, rings, gauds, conceits,
  Knacks, trifles, nosegays, sweetmeats—messengers
  Of strong prevailment in unhardened youth.
  With cunning hast thou filched my daughter's heart,
  Turned her obedience, which is due to me,
  To stubborn harshness. And my gracious duke,
  Be it so she will not here before your grace
  Consent to marry with Demetrius,   40
  I beg the ancient privilege of Athens.
  As she is mine, I may dispose of her:
  Which shall be either to this gentleman,
  Or to her death, according to our law
  Immediately provided in that case.
THESEUS: What say you Hermia? Be advised fair maid.
  To you your father should be as a god;

51 *figure*, impression, shape.

54 *in this kind*, i.e. as a husband.

58 *I . . . me.* Any movement or gesture? Is Hermia desperate, distraught, passionate, calm, tense, hysterical, defiant?

65–6 *Either . . . men.* How does Hermia respond to this?
65 *abjure*, renounce, give up, i.e. by entering a sisterhood.

68 *Know of*, consider. *examine . . . blood*, take your feelings into account.
70 *livery*, (a) distinctive dress, (b) servitude, calling.
71 *mewed*, shut up, enclosed.

74–5 *master . . . maiden.* What effect has this balanced contrast—emphasis, clarity, compression, memorableness?
74 *blood*, natural feelings.
70–5 What effect has the sequence of words associated with religion?
76 *rose distilled*, (a) the flower whose essence of beauty and fragrance is distilled, (b) the woman who passes on her beauty to the children she bears.

This thought occurs in other writers of the period, but Shakespeare seems particularly attracted by it. See *Sonnets*, 1, 5, and 6. The rose traditionally symbolized virginity and fading beauty.
78 *single*, i.e. alone, unmarried.
80 *patent*, right of ownership.

One that composed your beauties; yea and one
To whom you are but as a form in wax
By him imprinted, and within his power   50
To leave the figure or disfigure it.
Demetrius is a worthy gentleman.
HERMIA: So is Lysander.
THESEUS: In himself he is,
   But in this kind, wanting your father's voice,
   The other must be held the worthier.
HERMIA: I would my father looked but with my eyes.
THESEUS: Rather your eyes must with his judgement look.
HERMIA: I do entreat your grace to pardon me.
   I know not by what power I am made bold,
   Nor how it may concern my modesty   60
   In such a presence here to plead my thoughts.
   But I beseech your grace that I may know
   The worst that may befall me in this case,
   If I refuse to wed Demetrius.
THESEUS: Either to die the death, or to abjure
   For ever the society of men.
   Therefore, fair Hermia, question your desires,
   Know of your youth, examine well your blood,
   Whether, if you yield not to your father's choice,
   You can endure the livery of a nun,   70
   For aye to be in shady cloister mewed,
   To live a barren sister all your life,
   Chanting faint hymns to the cold fruitless moon.
   Thrice-blessed they that master so their blood,
   To undergo such maiden pilgrimage.
   But earthlier happy is the rose distilled,
   Than that which withering on the virgin thorn
   Grows, lives, and dies in single blessedness.
HERMIA: So will I grow, so live, so die, my lord,
   Ere I will yield my virgin patent up   80

81   *his lordship*, the rule of him.

      Is Hermia defiant, tearful, impertinent, contemptuous, restrained, over-emphatic, dignified?

88   *as he would*, as he wishes you to do.

89   *protest*, vow.

92   *crazed title*, unsound claim. *certain*, undoubted, established.

95   *Scornful*. Is Lysander mocking, scornful, flippant, contemptuous, fierce, jesting, bitter?

98   *estate unto*, grant to.

99–   *I . . . man*. Is Lysander—indignant, proud, pleading, contemptu-
110   ous, anguished?

      Any movement or gesture?

99   *well derived*, well born, of good family.

100   *possessed*, provided with worldly goods.

101   *fairly ranked*, equal in standing.

102   *If . . . vantage*, if not superior to.

105   *prosecute*, pursue, follow up.

106   *avouch . . . head*, declare it to his face.

106– *Demetrius . . . man*. Does Demetrius react to this accusation by any
10   movement or gesture?

108–9 *dotes . . . idolatry*, i.e. is completely infatuated with, utterly worships.

108   *dotes*, loves foolishly.

110   *spotted*, wicked.

Unto his lordship, whose unwished yoke
My soul consents not to give sovereignty.
THESEUS: Take time to pause, and, by the next new moon—
    The sealing-day betwixt my love and me,
    For everlasting bond of fellowship—
    Upon that day either prepare to die
    For disobedience to your father's will,
    Or else to wed Demetrius, as he would,
    Or on Diana's altar to protest
    For aye austerity and single life.   90
DEMETRIUS: Relent, sweet Hermia: and, Lysander, yield
    Thy crazed title to my certain right.
LYSANDER: You have her father's love, Demetrius;
    Let me have Hermia's. Do you marry him.
EGEUS: Scornful Lysander, true, he hath my love,
    And what is mine my love shall render him.
    And she is mine, and all my right of her
    I do estate unto Demetrius.
LYSANDER: I am my lord, as well derived as he,
    As well possessed. My love is more than his;   100
    My fortunes every way as fairly ranked,
    If not with vantage, as Demetrius';
    And, which is more than all these boasts can be,
    I am beloved of beauteous Hermia.
    Why should not I then prosecute my right?
    Demetrius, I'll avouch it to his head,
    Made love to Nedar's daughter, Helena,
    And won her soul; and she, sweet lady, dotes,
    Devoutly dotes, dotes in idolatry,
    Upon this spotted and inconstant man.   110
THESEUS: I must confess that I have heard so much,
    And with Demetrius thought to have spoke thereof;
    But being over-full of self affairs,
    My mind did lose it. But Demetrius come,

37

116   *schooling*, giving of instructions.
117   *arm*, prepare.
118   *fit your fancies*, make your wishes fit in with.

122   *Come . . . love?* What gestures are appropriate to express Theseus'
      tenderness? Is Hippolyta bored, day-dreaming, depressed, pensive,
      sad?
125   *Against*, in readiness for.
126   *nearly that*, that closely.

128–9 *How . . . fast?* An odd question after what has happened to
      Hermia. Perhaps it is a display of tenderness or of encouragement.
      Any movement?
130–1 *Belike . . . eyes.* Is this bitter, grim, spirited, playful, gallant, ironic?
131   *Beteem*, (*a*) grant, (*b*) pour (like rain).

133   *history*, story.

135– *either . . . eyes.* What is the effect of this alternating statement and
  40   comment, or kind of antiphon—to stress the mood of misery, to
      show their harmony with each other, to make them faintly
      ridiculous, to comfort themselves?
135   *blood*, birth, rank
136   *cross*, something that thwarts.
137   *misgraffed*, badly-joined, ill-matched.
138   *engaged*, pledged.
140   *O . . . eyes*, i.e. their predicament and hence the worst.
141   *sympathy*, mutual love.

143   *momentany*, momentary.

145   *collied*, black.
146   *spleen*, sudden passion or impulse.

And come Egeus, you shall go with me,
I have some private schooling for you both.
For you fair Hermia, look you arm yourself
To fit your fancies to your father's will;
Or else the law of Athens yields you up—
Which by no means we may extenuate—   120
To death, or to a vow of single life.
Come my Hippolyta, what cheer my love?
Demetrius and Egeus go along,
I must employ you in some business
Against our nuptial, and confer with you
Of something nearly that concerns yourselves.
EGEUS: With duty and desire we follow you.
                    [*Exeunt all but Lysander and Hermia*
LYSANDER: How now my love? Why is your cheek so pale?
How chance the roses there do fade so fast?
HERMIA: Belike for want of rain, which I could well   130
Beteem them from the tempest of my eyes.
LYSANDER: Ay me! For aught that I could ever read,
Could ever hear by tale or history,
The course of true love never did run smooth;
But either it was different in blood—
HERMIA: O cross! Too high to be enthralled to low.
LYSANDER: Or else misgraffed in respect of years—
HERMIA: O spite! Too old to be engaged to young.
LYSANDER: Or else it stood upon the choice of friends—
HERMIA: O hell! To choose love by another's eyes.   140
LYSANDER: Or, if there were a sympathy in choice,
War, death, or sickness did lay siege to it,
Making it momentany as a sound,
Swift as a shadow, short as any dream;
Brief as the lightning in the collied night,
That, in a spleen, unfolds both heaven and earth,
And ere a man hath power to say 'Behold!'

149   *confusion*, destruction, ruin.

Lysander's speech is the climax of despair. Has his description of love in 'tale or history' any truth?

150–5 *If . . . followers*. Is Hermia courageous, patient, sensible, practical, serene, depressed?

151   *edict in destiny*, law of fate.

152   *teach . . . patience*, teach ourselves patience to endure our trial.

155   *fancy's*, love's.

160   *respects*, regards, looks upon.

161–3 *There . . . us*. Any response from Hermia?

167   *do . . . May*, celebrate May-day dawn. These celebrations occurred not only on May Day but at any time during the summer.

169   *I . . . thee*. A mock serious gesture.

170   *arrow . . . head*. The arrow that aroused love by contrast with tha t of lead which provoked hatred.

171   *simplicity . . . doves*. This . . . may carry scriptural overtones from *St. Matthew*, *x*. 16: 'Simple as doves' (Rheims Version), Vulgate has 'simplices sicut columbae'. Hermia is perhaps playfully ironic. *simplicity*, innocence.

172   *that . . . loves*. Perhaps a reference to the girdle of Venus said to arouse love for the wearer.

173–4 *fire . . . seen*. In Virgil's *Æneid*, Æneas, escaping from the destruction of Troy landed at Carthage. Dido, Queen of Carthage, fell in love with him and he with her. Æneas, however, obedient to Jupiter's commands left Carthage by night for Italy. Dido in despair built a funeral pyre and died in its flames.

Are the things Hermia swears by—unreliable, playfully intended, seriously considered, symbols of romantic love, of falseness, or of infatuation?

What is her mood—gay, passionate, exhilarated, spirited, teasing, intense, witty, mimicking?

The jaws of darkness do devour it up.
So quick bright things come to confusion.
HERMIA: If then true lovers have been ever crossed,   150
    It stands as an edict in destiny.
    Then let us teach our trial patience,
    Because it is a customary cross,
    As due to love, as thoughts and dreams and sighs,
    Wishes and tears, poor fancy's followers.
LYSANDER: A good persuasion. Therefore hear me, Hermia.
    I have a widow aunt, a dowager
    Of great revenue, and she hath no child;
    From Athens is her house remote seven leagues,
    And she respects me as her only son.   160
    There, gentle Hermia, may I marry thee;
    And to that place the sharp Athenian law
    Cannot pursue us. If thou lovest me then,
    Steal forth thy father's house tomorrow night,
    And in the wood, a league without the town,
    Where I did meet thee once with Helena,
    To do observance to a morn of May,
    There will I stay for thee.
HERMIA: My good Lysander,
    I swear to thee by Cupid's strongest bow,
    By his best arrow with the golden head,   170
    By the simplicity of Venus' doves,
    By that which knitteth souls, and prospers loves,
    And by that fire which burned the Carthage queen,
    When the false Troyan under sail was seen,
    By all the vows that ever men have broke,
    In number more than ever women spoke,
    In that same place thou hast appointed me,
    Tomorrow truly will I meet with thee.
LYSANDER: Keep promise love. Look, here comes Helena.

180   *God speed*, may God bless you.

182   *fair*, (*a*) beauty, (*b*) beautiful woman.
183   *lode-stars*, i.e. men are attracted by them. *air*, sound, tone.
184   *tuneable*, tuneful.

186   *favour*, (*a*) love, (*b*) beauty, (*c*) perhaps a glance at 'fever'.

188   *ear . . . voice*, i.e. Helena's ear would receive the praise now given
      to Hermia.
190   *bated*, excepted.
191   *to . . . translated*, if I could be transformed to you.
192   *art*, magic art.
193   *sway the motion*, (*a*) control the beat, (*b*) rule the emotions.
194– *I . . . mine*. Another passage of alternating lines of dialogue with
  201   elaborate inversion of antitheses. What effect is intended—despair,
      infatuation, 'devoutly' doting, ridicule, grief, wilfulness?

206   *graces*, (*a*) attractive qualities, (*b*) divine influences.
      Helena sums up her bitterness as a paradox even as Hermia and
      Lysander had bewailed the contradictoriness of lovers' affairs.

209   *Phoebe*, In classical myth the goddess of the moon.
210   *glass*, mirror.

Enter HELENA

HERMIA: God speed fair Helena, whither away?   180
HELENA: Call you me fair? That fair again unsay.
Demetrius loves your fair. O happy fair!
Your eyes are lode-stars, and your tongue's sweet air
More tuneable than lark to shepherd's ear,
When wheat is green, when hawthorn buds appear.
Sickness is catching. O were favour so,
Yours would I catch, fair Hermia, ere I go,
My ear should catch your voice, my eye your eye,
My tongue should catch your tongue's sweet melody.
Were the world mine, Demetrius being bated,   190
The rest I'd give to be to you translated.
O teach me how you look, and with what art
You sway the motion of Demetrius' heart.
HERMIA: I frown upon him, yet he loves me still.
HELENA: O that your frowns would teach my smiles such skill.
HERMIA: I give him curses, yet he gives me love.
HELENA: O that my prayers could such affection move.
HERMIA: The more I hate, the more he follows me.
HELENA: The more I love, the more he hateth me.
HERMIA: His folly, Helena, is no fault of mine.   200
HELENA: None but your beauty; would that fault were mine.
HERMIA: Take comfort. He no more shall see my face,
Lysander and myself will fly this place.
Before the time I did Lysander see,
Seemed Athens as a paradise to me.
O then, what graces in my love do dwell,
That he hath turned a heaven unto a hell.
LYSANDER: Helen, to you our minds we will unfold:
Tomorrow night, when Phoebe doth behold
Her silver visage in the watery glass,   210
Decking with liquid pearl the bladed grass—

212   *still*, always.

216   *Emptying . . . sweet*, pouring out to each other our precious inmost thoughts.

219   *companies*, companions.

223   *lovers' food*, i.e. the sight of the loved one.
         Any parting gestures between Hermia and Lysander?

232   *quantity*, worth, substance, proportion.

240   *waggish*, mischievous, merry.
241   *So . . . everywhere*. See ll. 132–40.

243   *hailed*, (*a*) showered, (*b*) called (heaven to witness).

A time that lovers' flights doth still conceal—
Through Athens' gates have we devised to steal.
HERMIA: And in the wood, where often you and I
Upon faint primrose-beds were wont to lie,
Emptying our bosoms of their counsel sweet,
There my Lysander and myself shall meet;
And thence from Athens turn away our eyes
To seek new friends and stranger companies.
Farewell, sweet playfellow; pray thou for us,   220
And good luck grant thee thy Demetrius.
Keep word Lysander, we must starve our sight
From lovers' food till morrow deep midnight.
LYSANDER: I will my Hermia.   [*Exit Hermia*
              Helena adieu.
As you on him, Demetrius dote on you.   [*Exit*
HELENA: How happy some o'er other some can be!
Through Athens I am thought as fair as she.
But what of that? Demetrius thinks not so.
He will not know what all but he do know;
And as he errs, doting on Hermia's eyes,   230
So I, admiring of his qualities.
Things base and vile, holding no quantity,
Love can transpose to form and dignity.
Love looks not with the eyes, but with the mind,
And therefore is winged Cupid painted blind.
Nor hath Love's mind of any judgement taste;
Wings and no eyes figure unheedy haste.
And therefore is Love said to be a child,
Because in choice he is so oft beguiled.
As waggish boys in game themselves forswear,   240
So the boy Love is perjured everywhere.
For ere Demetrius looked on Hermia's eyne,
He hailed down oaths that he was only mine;
And when this hail some heat from Hermia felt,

245   *dissolved*, (*a*) broke his oaths, (*b*) melted (with love). See IV. i, 163.

246-8 *I . . . her*. Any change in pitch of voice or speed of speaking?

248   *intelligence*, information.

249   *dear expense*, (*a*) painful (dire) cost, (*b*) costly price to pay.

250   *enrich*. A continuation of the image in 'dear expense', but with the paradoxical turn that the loss is gain. *pain*, refers to 'dear' ('dire') as well as to her love anguish.

251   *his*, of him.

From l. 171 the dialogue is in couplets. What is their dramatic value—a more appropriate verse form for romance and lovers, to induce a kind of incantatory effect, to lead to the unreality of the events in the wood?

Are the three lovers—silly, sentimental, loyal, infatuated, wise, melancholy, self-deceived, reckless, selfish, adolescent, immature ?

Peter Quince's House

Should the 'mechanicals' enter together or variously? Should they be dressed in accordance with their trades? (See *Julius Cæsar*, I. i, 3–5)

s.D.   *Quince*. Explained by Dover Wilson as a spelling of 'quoins', wooden wedges used by carpenters. *Bottom*. The core on which woollen threads were wound. *Snug*, *Flute* and *Snout* are appropriate names for their trades. *Starveling* may refer to the proverbial weakness of tailors, of whom it took nine to make a man; alternatively it may refer to their supposed habit of 'starving' their customers of the material given them to make garments.

1   *company*, (*a*) actors' company–a somewhat flattering description, (*b*) fellows.

2   *generally*. Bottom means 'severally' (individually).

3   *scrip*, list of parts.

5   *interlude*, short play.

6   *on . . . night*. One of the slightly tilted, amusing oddities that occur in the mechanicals' speeches. See l. 20, 'look to their eyes'.

8   *grow . . . point*, come to the point.

9-10 *The . . . Thisby*. Such titles did in fact occur. The best known is that of the 'Comedy' of *King Cambises*: 'A Lamentable Tragedy mixed full of Pleasant Mirth'.

9   *comedy*. The word described plays that were not tragedies, i.e. did

So he dissolved, and showers of oaths did melt.
I will go tell him of fair Hermia's flight.
Then to the wood will he tomorrow night
Pursue her; and for this intelligence
If I have thanks, it is a dear expense.
But herein mean I to enrich my pain,   250
To have his sight thither and back again.   [*Exit*

SCENE TWO

Enter QUINCE, SNUG, BOTTOM, FLUTE, SNOUT, *and*
STARVELING

QUINCE: Is all our company here?

BOTTOM: You were best to call them generally, man by man,
according to the scrip.

QUINCE: Here is the scroll of every man's name, which is
thought fit, through all Athens, to play in our interlude before
the duke and the duchess, on his wedding-day at night.

BOTTOM: First good Peter Quince, say what the play treats on,
then read the names of the actors, and so grow to a point.

QUINCE: Marry, our play is, 'The most lamentable comedy, and

not involve the death of the principal character. Bottom, however, takes it as mirth provoking.

10   *Pyramus and Thisby*. See Appendix I, p. 175.

13   *spread yourselves*. What movements lead up to this? How do they spread themselves?

17   *lover . . . tyrant*. Two popular stage characters exemplified by the heroes of romances and by such a tyrant as Herod.

20   *look . . . eyes*. A happy ambiguity!

21–2 *my chief humour,* I am by temperament more suited.

22   *Ercles*, Hercules. The stage characters Hercules and Herod were notorious for their roaring and ranting 'to split the ears of the groundlings'. Some editors see in this a sly dig at Alleyn, the chief actor in the rival company of actors. He frequently played the part of a tyrant. *rarely*, excellently.

23   *to . . . in*, to rage fiercely. *split*, i.e. with fear.

24–31 *The . . . Fates*. Some see a parody of some lines in Jasper Heywood's translation of Seneca's play, *Hercules Furens*. Sharpe, *Real War of the Theatres*, thinks that Shakespeare was parodying Thomas Heywood's play *The Silver Age*.

27   *prison gates*. Possibly the gates of Hades. The myth of Hercules tells how for his twelfth labour he descended to Hades to capture the three-headed dog Cerberus. He found Theseus bound to a rock and tore him free.

28   *Phibbus' car*. In Ovid's stories Phoebus, the sun-god, drove the chariot of the sun daily across the heavens. Is this declamation supported by gestures, attitudes or poses?

32   *lofty*, high sounding.

33   *condoling*. Bottom means expressive of grief.

35   *Flute*. How should Flute pitch his voice?

37   *a wandering knight*, i.e. a knight-errant, a figure in the popular romances of the time. Shakespeare is perhaps poking gentle fun at the tastes of the unlearned.

39–40 *Nay . . . coming*. How should this be said—proudly, shyly, coyly, hesitatingly? Any response from the others?

48

most cruel death of Pyramus and Thisby'.   10
BOTTOM: A very good piece of work I assure you, and a merry.
Now good Peter Quince, call forth your actors by the scroll.
Masters, spread yourselves.
QUINCE: Answer as I call you. Nick Bottom the weaver.
BOTTOM: Ready. Name what part I am for, and proceed.
QUINCE: You, Nick Bottom, are set down for Pyramus.
BOTTOM: What is Pyramus? A lover, or a tyrant?
QUINCE: A lover that kills himself most gallant for love.
BOTTOM: That will ask some tears in the true performing of it.
If I do it, let the audience look to their eyes; I will move storms,
I will condole in some measure. To the rest. Yet my chief
humour is for a tyrant; I could play Ercles rarely, or a part to
tear a cat in, to make all split.   23

> The raging rocks,
> And shivering shocks
> Shall break the locks
>   Of prison gates;
> And Phibbus' car
> Shall shine from far,
> And make and mar   30
>   The foolish Fates.

This was lofty. Now name the rest of the players. This is
Ercles' vein, a tyrant's vein. A lover is more condoling.
QUINCE: Francis Flute the bellows-mender.
FLUTE: Here Peter Quince.
QUINCE: Flute, you must take Thisby on you.
FLUTE: What is Thisby? A wandering knight?
QUINCE: It is the lady that Pyramus must love.
FLUTE: Nay faith, let not me play a woman, I have a beard
coming.   40

43   *An*, if.

44   *monstrous*, (*a*) enormously, (*b*) unnaturally, (*c*) extremely. *Thisne, Thisne*. Bottom first as Pyramus calls Thisby's name endearingly and then in a 'monstrous little voice' replies 'Ah Pyramus, etc.'. Some editors prefer to take 'Thisne' as 'thissen', i.e. thus, in this way.

48   *Well, proceed*. Is Bottom sulky, mollified, resentful, indifferent?

51   *Thisby's mother*. This part together with those of Pyramus' father and Thisby's father is not heard of again. How is this casting received?

56–7   *Have . . . study*. What pitch of voice and speed of delivery are appropriate?

62–4   *An . . . all*. See note to III. 1, 28.

66–68   *I . . . us*. Is Bottom sarcastic, on his dignity, contemptuous, logical, sneering, good humoured?

68   *aggravate*, (*a*) add weight to, (*b*) make worse. What did Bottom mean?

69   *sucking*, young.

72   *proper*, handsome.

72–3   *see . . . day*, i.e. under the most favourable circumstances. A proverbial expression.

73–74   *you . . . Pyramus*. Is Quince subtle, cunning, worried, flattering, kindly? How does Bottom respond—reluctantly, complacently, preening himself, surlily, after consideration? What are the others doing at this time?

QUINCE That's all one. You shall play it in a mask, and you may speak as small as you will.

BOTTOM: An I may hide my face, let me play Thisby too. I'll speak in a monstrous little voice, 'Thisne, Thisne'. 'Ah Pyramus, my lover dear, thy Thisby dear, and lady dear.'

QUINCE: No no; you must play Pyramus, and Flute, you Thisby.

BOTTOM: Well, proceed.

QUINCE: Robin Starveling the tailor.

STARVELING: Here Peter Quince.   50

QUINCE: Robin Starveling, you must play Thisby's mother. Tom Snout the tinker.

SNOUT: Here Peter Quince.

QUINCE: You, Pyramus' father; myself, Thisby's father; Snug the joiner, you the lion's part. And, I hope, here is a play fitted.

SNUG: Have you the lion's part written? Pray you, if it be, give it me, for I am slow of study.

QUINCE: You may do it extempore, for it is nothing but roaring.

BOTTOM: Let me play the lion too. I will roar, that I will do any man's heart good to hear me. I will roar, that I will make the duke say, 'Let him roar again, let him roar again'.   61

QUINCE: An you should do it too terribly, you would fright the duchess, and the ladies, that they would shriek, and that were enough to hang us all.

ALL: That would hang us, every mother's son.

BOTTOM: I grant you, friends, if that you should fright the ladies out of their wits, they would have no more discretion but to hang us; but I will aggravate my voice so, that I will roar you as gently as any sucking dove; I will roar you an 'twere any nightingale.   70

QUINCE: You can play no part but Pyramus, for Pyramus is a sweet-faced man, a proper man as one shall see in a summer's day; a most lovely, gentleman-like man: therefore you must needs play Pyramus.

78–80 *straw-colour . . . yellow*. Bottom 'rattles off the names of various dyes familiar to him in his craft' (Wilson).

79 *in-grain*, fast dyed.

80 *perfect yellow*, i.e. gold colour.

81 *French crowns*, (*a*) gold coins, (*b*) bald heads, the result of French or venereal disease.

82 *barefaced*. Any appreciation from the others of Quince's joke? *parts*, the actors' scripts written out with cues.

83 *entreat . . . desire*. Is Quince hesitant, emphatic, imploring? *con*, learn.

86 *dogged*, followed.

87 *devices*, plans.

89–90 *obscenely*, (*a*) unseen and obscurely, (*b*) in inappropriate style (rhetorical). Perhaps a hint to the audience what to expect. See *Love's Labour's Lost*, IV. i, 136.

90 *courageously*, in good heart, without fear of being followed.

92 *Hold . . . bow-strings*. A proverbial expression meaning at all events, under any circumstances.

Is Bottom puerile, conceited, enthusiastic, blundering, boastful, ignorant, warm-hearted, self-willed, easily led?

BOTTOM: Well, I will undertake it. What beard were I best to play it in?

QUINCE: Why, what you will.

BOTTOM: I will discharge it in either your straw-colour beard, your orange-tawny beard, your purple-in-grain beard, or your French-crown-colour beard, your perfect yellow.   80

QUINCE: Some of your French crowns have no hair at all, and then you will play barefaced. But masters, here are your parts, and I am to entreat you, request you, and desire you, to con them by tomorrow night; and meet me in the palace wood, a mile without the town, by moonlight; there will we rehearse. For if we meet in the city, we shall be dogged with company, and our devices known. In the meantime I will draw a bill of properties, such as our play wants. I pray you fail me not.

BOTTOM: We will meet, and there we may rehearse most ob-scenely and courageously. Take pains, be perfect. Adieu.   90

QUINCE: At the duke's oak we meet.

BOTTOM: Enough. Hold or cut bow-strings.   *[Exeunt*

A wood near Athens

Does Puck alarm the Fairy, do they meet quietly and sedately, or are both surprised or amused?

In another Elizabethan play Puck was dressed in a calf skin. How should the Fairy be dressed and equipped—flowing robes, wings, a wand, ordinary Elizabethan dress, skins? Is the Fairy male or female?

3   *Thorough*, through.
4   *Over . . . pale*, i.e. passing over boundaries and fences.
5   *flood*, water.
     What effect does the alliteration have?
7   *moon's sphere*. According to astronomical beliefs current in Shakespeare's time, the moon was fixed in a hollow, transparent ball which revolved round the earth.
9   *orbs*, fairy rings.
10–12 *pensioners . . . rubies*. An allusion to Queen Elizabeth's Gentlemen Pensioners, fifty young men selected for their handsome appearance, whose rich clothes were decorated with jewels and lace.
12   *fairy favours*, presents from the Fairy Queen.
13   *In . . . savours*. It was believed that the fragrance of cowslips came from the pink spots at the bottom of the flower-bell.
14 ff. Why does the verse change here—because ll. 2–13 were sung or chanted, because informative conversation begins here?
16   *lob*, clod-hopper. Is this contemptuous, impudent, mocking, playful?
18   *The . . . tonight*. Is Puck excited, indignant, amused, delighted?

20   *passing fell*, exceedingly angry.

ACT TWO

SCENE ONE

Enter a FAIRY *at one door, and* PUCK *at another*

PUCK: How now, spirit, whither wander you?
FAIRY: Over hill, over dale,
    Thorough bush, thorough brier,
  Over park, over pale,
    Thorough flood, thorough fire;
  I do wander every where,
  Swifter than the moon's sphere;
  And I serve the Fairy Queen,
  To dew her orbs upon the green.
  The cowslips tall her pensioners be,   10
  In their gold coats spots you see,
  Those be rubies, fairy favours,
  In those freckles live their savours.
  I must go seek some dewdrops here,
  And hang a pearl in every cowslip's ear.
  Farewell thou lob of spirits; I'll be gone.
  Our queen and all her elves come here anon.
PUCK: The king doth keep his revels here tonight.
  Take heed the queen come not within his sight.
  For Oberon is passing fell and wrath,   20
  Because that she, as her attendant, hath
  A lovely boy stolen from an Indian king.

23   *changeling*. It was believed that fairies stole human babies leaving a
      fairy child in their place. Usually the fairy substitute was called the
      changeling.

25   *Knight*, attendant.

29   *fountain*, spring, well.

30   *square*, quarrel, squabble.

33   *shrewd*, mischievous, impish.

36   *Skim milk*, i.e. steal the cream. *quern*, stone hand-mill for grinding
      pepper, mustard or corn.

37   *bootless . . . churn*. Milk sometimes needed a long churning before
      the butter appeared. Puck, it was believed, was responsible for the
      delay. *bootless*, in vain.

38   *barm*, froth, i.e. the ale was flat, or the yeast would not work and
      the beer was spoilt.

41   *You . . . luck*. Another belief held that Puck did housework at
      night if kindly treated and provided with a bowl of milk.
          How does Puck react to this description of his pranks—with
      solemnity, with chuckles or bursts of laughter, with capering or
      mimicking gestures?

45   *bean-fed horse*, i.e. a lusty stallion. Should Puck demonstrate any of
      these tricks?

46   *filly foal*, young mare.

47   *gossip's*, old woman's.

48   *roasted crab*, i.e. crab apple. The drink called 'lamb's wool' was
      made of hot ale with nutmeg and sugar. Hot roasted crab apples
      were added.

50   *dewlap*, loose fold of flesh at the throat.

51   *aunt*, old woman.

54   *And . . . cough*. Various interpretations have been suggested—the
      faller squats like a tailor, or takes a 'tailer' by analogy with
      'header'. Mrs. Hulme cites the proverb, 'His tail will catch the kin-
      cough', said of one who sits on the ground (kin-cough = whoop-
      ing cough).

55   *quire*, chorus, noisy company.

She never had so sweet a changeling.
And jealous Oberon would have the child
Knight of his train, to trace the forests wild.
But she perforce withholds the loved boy,
Crowns him with flowers, and makes him all her joy.
And now they never meet in grove, or green,
By fountain clear, or spangled starlight sheen,
But they do square, that all their elves for fear   30
Creep into acorn-cups, and hide them there.
FAIRY: Either I mistake your shape and making quite,
    Or else you are that shrewd and knavish sprite
    Called Robin Goodfellow. Are not you he,
    That frights the maidens of the villagery,
    Skim milk, and sometimes labour in the quern,
    And bootless make the breathless housewife churn,
    And sometime make the drink to bear no barm,
    Mislead night-wanderers, laughing at their harm?
    Those, that Hobgoblin call you, and sweet Puck,   40
    You do their work, and they shall have good luck.
    Are not you he?
PUCK: Thou speak'st aright;
    I am that merry wanderer of the night.
    I jest to Oberon and make him smile,
    When I a fat and bean-fed horse beguile,
    Neighing in likeness of a filly foal;
    And sometimes lurk I in a gossip's bowl,
    In very likeness of a roasted crab,
    And when she drinks, against her lips I bob,
    And on her withered dewlap pour the ale.   50
    The wisest aunt, telling the saddest tale,
    Sometimes for three-foot stool mistaketh me;
    Then slip I from her bum, down topples she,
    And 'tailor' cries, and falls into a cough;
    And then the whole quire hold their hips and laugh,

56   *waxen*, increase. *neeze*, sneeze, or snort, breathe heavily.

58–9   *But . . . gone.* What actions are appropriate?

60–   Apart from a few rhymes to mark exits these lines are blank
246   verse. Any reason for this?

62   *forsworn*, forsaken.

63   *wanton*, rebellious woman.

64   *Then . . . lady.* A mocking retort, perhaps emphasized by a
       curtsy, followed by accusations that there have been occasions
       when someone else has been his lady.

66   *Corin*, i.e. a shepherd. In the fashionable, pastoral stories and poetry
       of the period the chief figures were shepherds or were disguised as
       shepherds. Corin and Phillida are two names typical of lovers in
       these stories or poems.

67   *of corn*, of oat straw. Perhaps reeds were used. *versing love*, making
       love-songs.

69   *steep*, mountain-slope.

70   *forsooth*. Scornful. *bouncing*, big and brawny.

71   *buskined*, wearing the footwear of a hunter.
       'bouncing', 'buskined', 'warrior'. Titania is scornful of such a
       masculine woman.

72–3   Is Titania sarcastic, derisory, scornful, ironic?

75   *Glance . . . credit*, jeer at my honourable dealings.

78   *Perigenia*. The daughter of Sinnis, the robber, whom Theseus
       slew.

79   *Ægles*. The daughter of Panopeus for love of whom Theseus
       deserted Ariadne according to some legends.

80   *Ariadne*. The daughter of King Minos of Crete. With a reel of
       thread she helped Theseus to escape from the maze after he had
       killed the Minotaur. She eloped with him, but he left her on the
       isle of Naxos. *Antiopa*. Queen of the Amazons in another version
       of Theseus' relations with this tribe. It was admitted that Theseus'
       love affairs were, in fact, not to his credit. Shakespeare, following
       Chaucer's characterization of Theseus as magnanimous and
       chivalrous, suggests through Oberon that in addition Theseus has
       been misled by Titania.

81   *forgeries*, lying inventions.

82   *middle summer's spring*, beginning of midsummer.

86   *ringlets*, fairy rings.

And waxen in their mirth, and neeze, and swear
A merrier hour was never wasted there.
But room fairy, here comes Oberon.
FAIRY: And here my mistress. Would that he were gone.

Enter OBERON *at one door, with his train; and*
TITANIA *at another, with hers*

OBERON: Ill met by moonlight, proud Titania.   60
TITANIA: What, jealous Oberon? Fairies, skip hence.
I have forsworn his bed and company.
OBERON: Tarry, rash wanton. Am not I thy lord?
TITANIA: Then I must be thy lady. But I know
When thou hast stolen away from fairy land,
And in the shape of Corin sat all day,
Playing on pipes of corn, and versing love
To amorous Phillida. Why art thou here,
Come from the farthest steep of India?
But that, forsooth, the bouncing Amazon,   70
Your buskined mistress, and your warrior love,
To Theseus must be wedded; and you come
To give their bed joy and prosperity.
OBERON: How canst thou thus for shame, Titania,
Glance at my credit with Hippolyta,
Knowing I know thy love to Theseus?
Didst thou not lead him through the glimmering night
From Perigenia, whom he ravished?
And make him with fair Ægles break his faith,
With Ariadne, and Antiopa?   80
TITANIA: These are the forgeries of jealousy.
And never, since the middle summer's spring,
Met we on hill, in dale, forest, or mead,
By paved fountain, or by rushy brook,
Or in the beached margent of the sea,
To dance our ringlets to the whistling wind,

90   *Contagious fogs.* Fogs and certain winds were thought to bring diseases.

91   *pelting*, rushing. *proud*, swollen.

92   *continents*, banks.

93   *stretched*, tugged at, pulled.

94–5   *corn . . . beard*, i.e. barley.

97   *murrion flock*, dead, diseased sheep.

98   *nine men's morris.* A game for two players each of whom had nine men or pegs. Three concentric squares were traced in the turf with holes at the corners and middles of the sides. Each player tried to capture one of his opponent's men by moving his own men from one hole to another to arrange three of them in a straight line.

99   *mazes*, winding paths, or marks made by country dancers. *wanton*, coarse grown.

101   *cheer.* Quartos and Folios have 'heere' which some editors print. Others prefer 'gear'. Graphically 'heere' for 'cheere' is a possible error.

103–5 *Therefore . . . abound.* Is the moon angry because of (*a*) the quarrel, (*b*) the action of the winds, (*c*) the flooding of the rivers, (*d*) the lack of hymns or carols?

105   *rheumatic diseases*, diseases producing watery discharges from the nose and eyes, colds.

106   *distemperature*, disorder of nature.

109   *Hiems'*, Winter's. *thin*, scantily haired.

112   *childing*, fruitful.

113   *wonted liveries*, usual appearances. *mazed*, amazed.

114   *increase*, products.

116   *debate*, strife, quarrel.

117   *original*, origin, source.

      Titania describes the effect of their quarrel in bringing to nothing the livelihood, pastime, and worship of humans, and the confusion of the seasons—discord in royal fairy marriage gives birth to distressful offspring, underlined by such words as 'childing'—'increase'—'original'—'parents'.

      What is the point of this description—to establish the position of Oberon and Titania as gods, to bring things near to the audience's experience, to stress an aspect of marriage relationships?

But with thy brawls thou hast disturbed our sport.
Therefore the winds, piping to us in vain,
As in revenge, have sucked up from the sea
Contagious fogs; which falling in the land,   90
Hath every pelting river made so proud,
That they have overborne their continents.
The ox hath therefore stretched his yoke in vain,
The ploughman lost his sweat, and the green corn
Hath rotted ere his youth attained a beard.
The fold stands empty in the drowned field,
And crows are fatted with the murrion flock;
The nine men's morris is filled up with mud,
And the quaint mazes in the wanton green,
For lack of tread, are undistinguishable.   100
The human mortals want their winter cheer,
No night is now with hymn or carol blest.
Therefore the moon, the governess of floods,
Pale in her anger, washes all the air,
That rheumatic diseases do abound.
And thorough this distemperature we see
The seasons alter; hoary-headed frosts
Fall in the fresh lap of the crimson rose,
And on old Hiems' thin and icy crown
An odorous chaplet of sweet summer buds   110
Is, as in mockery, set. The spring, the summer,
The childing autumn, angry winter, change
Their wonted liveries; and the mazed world,
By their increase, now knows not which is which.
And this same progeny of evils comes
From our debate, from our dissension;
We are their parents and original.
OBERON: Do you amend it then, it lies in you.
Why should Titania cross her Oberon?
I do but beg a little changeling boy,   120

121   *henchman,* squire, page of honour.

123   *vot'ress . . . order,* i.e. bound by vows to worship me. *order,* sisterhood.

127   *Marking,* watching. *traders,* merchantmen. *flood,* sea.
      What point has this recollection—to show Titania's preserving of natural fruitfulness, to contrast with the ill fruits of their quarrel, to show the happy, idyllic life of the fairies?
      Shakespeare frequently pictures love as rich merchandise, and the treasure of merchandise as the natural increase of children born in love.

139– *Perchance . . . haunts.* Is Titania petulant, carefree, playful, gener-
42   ous, whimsical?
140   *round,* round-dance.

149   *Since,* when.
150   *mermaid . . . back.* Possibly an allusion to one of the entertainments at Kenilworth when Elizabeth visited the Earl of Leicester there in 1575. See note to III. i, 38–40.
151   *breath,* voice, singing.
152   *rude,* (*a*) rough, (*b*) discourteous. *civil,* (*a*) gentle, (*b*) polite.

    To be my henchman.
TITANIA: Set your heart at rest,
  The fairy land buys not the child of me.
  His mother was a vot'ress of my order,
  And in the spiced Indian air, by night,
  Full often hath she gossiped by my side,
  And sat with me on Neptune's yellow sands,
  Marking th' embarked traders on the flood;
  When we have laughed to see the sails conceive,
  And grow big-bellied with the wanton wind;
  Which she, with pretty and with swimming gait   130
  Following, her womb then rich with my young squire,
  Would imitate, and sail upon the land,
  To fetch me trifles, and return again,
  As from a voyage, rich with merchandise.
  But she, being mortal, of that boy did die,
  And for her sake do I rear up her boy,
  And for her sake I will not part with him.
OBERON: How long within this wood intend you stay?
TITANIA: Perchance till after Theseus' wedding-day.
  If you will patiently dance in our round,   140
  And see our moonlight revels, go with us;
  If not, shun me, and I will spare your haunts.
OBERON: Give me that boy, and I will go with thee.
TITANIA: Not for thy fairy kingdom. Fairies away,
  We shall chide downright, if I longer stay.
                           [*Exit Titania with her train*
OBERON: Well, go thy way. Thou shalt not from this grove.
  Till I torment thee for this injury.
  My gentle Puck come hither. Thou remembrest
  Since once I sat upon a promontory,
  And heard a mermaid, on a dolphin's back,   150
  Uttering such dulcet and harmonious breath,
  That the rude sea grew civil at her song,

153 *stars . . . spheres.* Some editors, less plausibly, see a reference here to the firework displays given at entertainments presented to Elizabeth.

155 *but. . . not.* Is this—to show Puck's inferiority, to isolate and elevate a complimentary reference to Queen Elizabeth, to make an excuse for giving Puck information intended for the audience?

157 *Cupid all armed,* i.e. with golden-headed arrows. *certain,* sure, deadly.

158 *fair . . . west.* Possibly an allusion to Queen Elizabeth. See also 'imperial vot'ress' l. 163. *vestal,* virgin.

164 *maiden meditation, fancy-free,* with thoughts untouched by love.

168 *love-in-idleness,* (*a*) heartsease, pansy, (*b*) sensual desire.

174 *leviathan,* sea-monster. (See *Psalms,* civ. 26.)

182 *soul,* very essence.

184 *another herb.* See IV. i, 70–1.

And certain stars shot madly from their spheres,
To hear the sea-maid's music.
PUCK: I remember.
OBERON: That very time I saw—but thou couldst not—
  Flying between the cold moon and the earth,
  Cupid all armed: a certain aim he took
  At a fair vestal, throned by the west,
  And loosed his love-shaft smartly from his bow,
  As it should pierce a hundred thousand hearts.   160
  But I might see young Cupid's fiery shaft
  Quenched in the chaste beams of the watery moon,
  And the imperial vot'ress passed on,
  In maiden meditation, fancy-free.
  Yet marked I where the bolt of Cupid fell.
  It fell upon a little western flower,
  Before, milk-white; now purple with love's wound,
  And maidens call it, love-in-idleness.
  Fetch me that flower; the herb I showed thee once.
  The juice of it on sleeping eyelids laid,   170
  Will make or man or woman madly dote
  Upon the next live creature that it sees.
  Fetch me this herb, and be thou here again
  Ere the leviathan can swim a league.
PUCK: I'll put a girdle round about the earth
  In forty minutes.   [*Exit*
OBERON: Having once this juice,
  I'll watch Titania when she is asleep,
  And drop the liquor of it in her eyes.
  The next thing then she waking looks upon,
  Be it on lion, bear, or wolf, or bull,   180
  On meddling monkey, or on busy ape,
  She shall pursue it with the soul of love.
  And ere I take this charm from off her sight—
  As I can take it with another herb—

186   *I am invisible.* Oberon may wrap a cloak or mantle round himself.

187   *conference,* conversation.

S.D.   Is Helena clinging to Demetrius, or following him closely? Is he thrusting her away, threatening her, turning towards her?

192   *wood,* (*a*) angry, mad, (*b*) perhaps wooed, tempted, and a glance at wood = forest. The pun perhaps indicates an explosive release of feeling.

194–5 *Hence . . . adamant.* Any movements or gestures?

195   *adamant,* (*a*) hardest stone, (*b*) lodestone, magnet.

196   *draw not iron,* i.e. as a lodestone does. Wilson suggests a quibble on 'iron' = sword.

199   *entice,* try to attract.

203–4 *I . . . on you.* Helena quotes a proverb to justify her actions. 'A woman, a spaniel, and a walnut tree, the more you beat them the better they be.' Is Helena nauseating, abject, despairing, true to life, humble, contemptuous, worthy, exasperating?

213   *And . . . you.* How should Demetrius receive this retort? *sick,* love-sick.

214   *impeach,* discredit, damage.

I'll make her render up her page to me.
But who comes here? I am invisible,
And I will overhear their conference.

Enter DEMETRIUS, HELENA *following him*

DEMETRIUS: I love thee not, therefore pursue me not.
　Where is Lysander, and fair Hermia?
　The one I'll slay, the other slayeth me.　　　　　　　190
　Thou told'st me they were stolen unto this wood;
　And here am I, and wood within this wood,
　Because I cannot meet my Hermia.
　Hence, get thee gone, and follow me no more.
HELENA: You draw me, you hard-hearted adamant;
　But yet you draw not iron, for my heart
　Is true as steel. Leave you your power to draw,
　And I shall have no power to follow you.
DEMETRIUS: Do I entice you? Do I speak you fair?
　Or rather do I not in plainest truth　　　　　　　　200
　Tell you I do not, nor I cannot love you?
HELENA: And even for that do I love you the more.
　I am your spaniel; and, Demetrius,
　The more you beat me, I will fawn on you.
　Use me but as your spaniel, spurn me, strike me,
　Neglect me, lose me; only give me leave,
　Unworthy as I am, to follow you.
　What worser place can I beg in your love,—
　And yet a place of high respect with me—
　Than to be used as you use your dog?　　　　　　　210
DEMETRIUS: Tempt not too much the hatred of my spirit,
　For I am sick when I do look on thee.
HELENA: And I am sick when I look not on you.
DEMETRIUS: You do impeach your modesty too much,
　To leave the city, and commit yourself
　Into the hands of one that loves you not,

218   *ill . . . place*, evil thoughts prompted by a deserted spot.

220   *privilege. For that*. This Q and F reading is emended by some editors to 'privilege for that'.

221   *It . . . face*, i.e. his presence drives away gloom of spirit. See Sonnet xliii 'All days are nights to see till I see thee, And nights bright days when dreams do show thee me'.

224   *all the world*, (*a*) everything that matters, (*b*) everybody in the world, (*c*) perhaps the audience.

       Is Helena—plaintive, witty, serious, maudlin, trusting, flattering, perceptive, clever, pitiful?

231   *Apollo . . . chase*. In classical myth Apollo, the sun-god, pursued the nymph Daphne. At her prayer for help her father, the river Peneus, changed her into a laurel.

232   *griffin*, a fabulous creature having the head and wings of an eagle and the body and hindquarters of a lion.

233   *Bootless*, vain, useless.

235   *let me go*. What actions are involved?

237   *mischief*, harm.

240   *do . . . sex*, make me do things that shame my sex, i.e. to woo him.

243   *make . . . hell*. A different kind of heaven from that in I. i, 205-7.

To trust the opportunity of night,
And the ill counsel of a desert place,
With the rich worth of your virginity.

HELENA: Your virtue is my privilege. For that   220
It is not night when I do see your face,
Therefore I think I am not in the night;
Nor doth this wood lack worlds of company,
For you in my respect are all the world.
Then how can it be said I am alone,
When all the world is here to look on me?

DEMETRIUS: I'll run from thee, and hide me in the brakes,
And leave thee to the mercy of wild beasts.

HELENA: The wildest hath not such a heart as you.
Run when you will. The story shall be changed: 230
Apollo flies, and Daphne holds the chase;
The dove pursues the griffin; the mild hind
Makes speed to catch the tiger. Bootless speed,
When cowardice pursues, and valour flies.

DEMETRIUS: I will not stay thy questions, let me go.
Or if thou follow me, do not believe
But I shall do thee mischief in the wood.   *[Exit Demetrius*

HELENA: Ay, in the temple, in the town, the field,
You do me mischief. Fie Demetrius,
Your wrongs do set a scandal on my sex.   240
We cannot fight for love, as men may do;
We should be wooed, and were not made to woo.
I'll follow thee, and make a heaven of hell,
To die upon the hand I love so well.   *[Exit Helena*

OBERON: Fare thee well nymph. Ere he do leave this grove,
Thou shalt fly him, and he shall seek thy love.

Enter PUCK

Hast thou the flower there? Welcome wanderer.

PUCK: Ay, there it is.

249– *I . . . fantasies.* Dover Wilson thinks that this was intended to be
58 sung, others disagree. These lines differ from those that follow in
rhyming and in having a thought completed in each line. Perhaps this passage in its rhythm and fragrant flower picture is
devised to fit the immortal Titania by contrast with the earthly
activities to be carried out by Puck on Demetrius.

249 *blows*, blooms.

250 *oxlips*, large cowslip-like flowers.

251 *luscious woodbine*, sweet honeysuckle.

252 *eglantine*, sweet-briar.

256 *Weed*, garment, robe.

258 *fantasies*, delusions.
How does Puck behave during Oberon's speech? Does he sit,
kneel, stand, grovel, roll in ecstasy, chuckle, shout 'Ho!'?

The wood

Titania's bower was possibly in the discovery space or in a canopied
space in front of the rear wall of the stage. What properties are required?
Should music accompany her entry? How should the fairy attendants
be grouped?

1 *roundel*, a round dance, accompanied here by the song, ll. 9–24.

3 *cankers*, maggots. *musk-rose*, briar rose.

4 *rere-mice*, bats.

6 *clamorous owl*, a bird whose cry foretold evil. *wonders*, i.e. stares
wonderingly.

OBERON: I pray thee give it me.
  I know a bank where the wild thyme blows,
  Where oxlips and the nodding violet grows, 250
  Quite over-canopied with luscious woodbine,
  With sweet musk-roses, and with eglantine.
  There sleeps Titania sometime of the night,
  Lulled in these flowers with dances and delight.
  And there the snake throws her enamelled skin,
  Weed wide enough to wrap a fairy in.
  And with the juice of this I'll streak her eyes,
  And make her full of hateful fantasies.
  Take thou some of it, and seek through this grove:
  A sweet Athenian lady is in love 260
  With a disdainful youth. Anoint his eyes,
  But do it when the next thing he espies
  May be the lady. Thou shalt know the man
  By the Athenian garments he hath on.
  Effect it with some care, that he may prove
  More fond on her than she upon her love.
  And look thou meet me ere the first cock crow.
PUCK: Fear not my lord, your servant shall do so.

[Exeunt

SCENE TWO

Enter TITANIA, *with her train*

TITANIA: Come, now a roundel and a fairy song;
  Then, for the third part of a minute, hence—
  Some to kill cankers in the musk-rose buds,
  Some war with rere-mice for their leathern wings,
  To make my small elves coats, and some keep back
  The clamorous owl, that nightly hoots and wonders

7   *quaint*, dainty.
8   *offices*, duties.

9–23   *You . . . offence*. Many of these creatures were associated with witchcraft, or evil, or were objects of fear. Some were ingredients in the witches' cauldron in *Macbeth*, IV. i.

11   *blind-worms*, slow worms.

13   *Philomel, with melody*. What effect has the symmetrical arrangement of the vowels and some consonants?

20   *spiders*. Regarded as poisonous.
     The dance and departure of the fairies should be carefully patterned.

S.D.   *Enter . . . eyelids*. Where is the sentinel?
     Is Oberon's entry stealthy, dignified, slinking, majestic?
     What effect is aimed at by the short lines and the two rhyming sounds—rapidity, spell, incantation, threat? Any movements or gestures?

At our quaint spirits. Sing me now asleep;
Then to your offices, and let me rest.

Fairies sing

FIRST FAIRY

You spotted snakes with double tongue,
   Thorny hedgehogs, be not seen, 10
Newts and blind-worms do no wrong,
   Come not near our Fairy Queen.
   Philomel, with melody,
   Sing in our sweet lullaby,
Lulla, lulla, lullaby, lulla, lulla, lullaby;
   Never harm,
   Nor spell, nor charm,
Come our lovely lady nigh.
So good night, with lullaby.

SECOND FAIRY

Weaving spiders come not here; 20
   Hence you long-legged spinners, hence.
Beetles black approach not near;
   Worm nor snail, do no offence.
   Philomel, with melody, &c.

FIRST FAIRY

Hence away, now all is well.
One aloof stand sentinel.

          [Exeunt Fairies. Titania sleeps

Enter OBERON, *and squeezes the flower on* TITANIA's *eyelids*

OBERON: What thou seest when thou dost wake,
       Do it for thy true-love take;
       Love and languish for his sake.
       Be it ounce, or cat, or bear, 30

31   *Pard*, leopard.

35   *Fair . . . wood*. Any action to support this?

45   *take . . . innocence*, take my meaning in the innocent way it is
     intended.
         Lysander puns on 'sense' and 'innocence' as a starting point for
     his argument.
46   *Love . . . conference*, 'love enables lovers to understand each other's
     true meaning' (Chambers).
49   *bosoms*, thoughts, feelings.
50   *troth*, pledge, truth.
52   *I . . . lie*, I am not false.

54   *beshrew . . . pride*, may my manners and my breeding be blamed.

59   *Becomes*, is fit for.

Pard, or boar with bristled hair,
In thy eye that shall appear
When thou wakest, it is thy dear.
Wake when some vile thing is near.   [*Exit*

Enter LYSANDER *and* HERMIA

LYSANDER: Fair love, you faint with wandering in the wood,
          And to speak troth I have forgot our way.
      We'll rest us Hermia, if you think it good,
      And tarry for the comfort of the day.
HERMIA: Be it so Lysander; find you out a bed,
    For I upon this bank will rest my head.   40
LYSANDER: One turf shall serve as pillow for us both,
    One heart, one bed, two bosoms, and one troth.
HERMIA: Nay good Lysander, for my sake, my dear,
    Lie further off yet, do not lie so near.
LYSANDER: O take the sense, sweet, of my innocence.
  Love takes the meaning in love's conference.
  I mean that my heart unto yours is knit,
  So that but one heart we can make of it.
  Two bosoms interchained with an oath;
  So then two bosoms, and a single troth.   50
  Then by your side no bed-room me deny;
  For lying so, Hermia, I do not lie.
HERMIA: Lysander riddles very prettily.
  Now much beshrew my manners and my pride,
  If Hermia meant to say Lysander lied.
  But gentle friend, for love and courtesy
  Lie further off, in human modesty;
  Such separation as may well be said
  Becomes a virtuous bachelor and a maid,
  So far be distant; and good night sweet friend.   60
  Thy love ne'er alter till thy sweet life end.
LYSANDER: Amen, amen, to that fair prayer, say I;

65   *With . . . pressed*. A playful sharing of benefits.

s.D.   Enter Puck. Should his entry be—athletic, stealthy, sudden, swift, light-footed, through a trap-door?

       Should he speak as if talking to himself or directly address the audience?

68   *approve*, test.

75   *dank*, damp.

76–7 *she . . . kill-courtesy*. An ironical comment on their modesty.

77   *Near . . . kill-courtesy*. Any action to show his disgust?

78   *Churl*, lout, ungracious fellow.

79   *owe*, possess.

80   *forbid*, i.e. that you have rejected.

81   *Sleep . . . eyelid*, i.e. let love-pangs drive away sleep from its natural place on Lysander's eyelids.

86   *O . . . so*. Helena is terrified of the dark. *darkling*, in the dark.

88   *fond*, (*a*) foolish, (*b*) loving.

89   *The . . . grace*, the more I plead with Demetrius the less favour he shows me.

       There is a quibble on the religious significance of 'prayer' and 'grace'.

And then end life when I end loyalty.
Here is my bed; sleep give thee all his rest.
HERMIA: With half that wish the wisher's eyes be pressed.
                                                    [*They sleep*

Enter PUCK

PUCK: Through the forest have I gone,
               But Athenian found I none,
               On whose eyes I might approve
               This flower's force in stirring love.
               Night and silence—Who is here?   70
               Weeds of Athens he doth wear.
               This is he, my master said,
               Despised the Athenian maid.
               And here the maiden, sleeping sound,
               On the dank and dirty ground.
               Pretty soul, she durst not lie
               Near this lack-love, this kill-courtesy.
               Churl, upon thy eyes I throw
                         [*Puts the juice on Lysander's eyelids*
               All the power this charm doth owe.
               When thou wakest, let love forbid   80
               Sleep his seat on thy eyelid.
               So awake when I am gone;
               For I must now to Oberon.   [*Exit*

Enter DEMETRIUS *and* HELENA, *running*

HELENA: Stay, though thou kill me, sweet Demetrius.
DEMETRIUS: I charge thee hence, and do not haunt me thus.
HELENA: O wilt thou darkling leave me? Do not so.
DEMETRIUS: Stay, on thy peril; I alone will go.   [*Exit*
HELENA: O, I am out of breath in this fond chase.
   The more my prayer, the lesser is my grace.
   Happy is Hermia, wheresoe'er she lies;   90

77

97   *as a monster*, as if I were a monster.

98   *dissembling*, deceitful.

99   *sphery eyne*, eyes like stars in their spheres (orbits).

103   *And . . . sake.* Any actions and movements?

104–5 *Transparent . . . heart.* A complex platonic thought perhaps prompted by Helena's name which means fire (torch or meteor). Angelic or divine nature was identified with fire which was transparent. The divine soul or idea in the perfect beauty inhabited a 'shrine of crystal flesh, through which to shine'. In Helena nature is thus reconciled and integrated with art.

104   *art*, (*a*) magic art, (*b*) painter's art.

106–7 *Demetrius . . . sword.* Spencer points out that 'vile name' is not inappropriate in the mouth of an Athenian. Plutarch describes the life of Demetrius Poliorcetes as a parallel to that of Marcus Antonius. Demetrius was an Athenian of a particularly vicious, debauched and lecherous character.

109   *Lord, what though?* Is this despairing, indignant, resigned, in alarm?

114   *raven.* The raven was a bird of ill omen. Dark hair was unfashionable among Elizabethan ladies. *raven . . . dove.* Perhaps a glance at the story of the flood.

115–   *The . . . will.* With considerable irony Lysander tries to ascribe the
20   effects of the love-juice to the maturing of his powers of reason.

115   *The . . . swayed.* Bottom pronounced a different opinion, III. i, 127–8.

118   *ripe not*, i.e. did not ripen.

119   *touching . . . skill*, reaching now the highest point of human understanding.

120   *marshal*, an officer who led royal processions.

121   *o'erlook*, read.

121–2 *eyes . . . book.* It was held that love began in the eyes. *See Love's Labour's Lost*, IV. iii, 346–9:

> 'From women's eyes this doctrine I derive.
>
> . . . .
>
> They are the books, the arts, the academes,
>
> That show, contain and nourish, all the world.'

Any exchanges of movement?

123   *born*, i.e. born to endure.

For she hath blessed and attractive eyes.
How came her eyes so bright? Not with salt tears;
If so, my eyes are oftener washed than hers.
No, no, I am as ugly as a bear,
For beasts that meet me run away for fear.
Therefore no marvel though Demetrius
Do, as a monster, fly my presence thus.
What wicked and dissembling glass of mine
Made me compare with Hermia's sphery eyne?
But who is here? Lysander, on the ground,   100
Dead, or asleep? I see no blood, no wound.
Lysander, if you live, good sir awake.

LYSANDER: [*Awaking*] And run through fire I will for thy sweet
    sake.
Transparent Helena, Nature shows art,
That through thy bosom makes me see thy heart.
Where is Demetrius? O how fit a word
Is that vile name to perish on my sword.

HELENA: Do not say so, Lysander, say not so.
What though he love your Hermia? Lord, what though?
Yet Hermia still loves you; then be content.   110

LYSANDER: Content with Hermia? No, I do repent
The tedious minutes I with her have spent.
Not Hermia, but Helena I love.
Who will not change a raven for a dove?
The will of man is by his reason swayed;
And reason says you are the worthier maid.
Things growing are not ripe until their season;
So I, being young, till now ripe not to reason;
And touching now the point of human skill,
Reason becomes the marshal to my will,   120
And leads me to your eyes, where I o'erlook
Love's stories, written in love's richest book.

HELENA: Wherefore was I to this keen mockery born?

125   *Is 't . . . man.* Is this prudish, grandmotherly, dignified, shrewish, caustic, contemptuous, indignant, petulant?

126   *nor never can.* Emphatic.

128   *flout,* mock. *insufficiency,* shortcomings, inadequacy.

129   *sooth,* truth.

133–4   *O . . . abused.* Does she depart in anger, despair, indignation, tears?

134   *abused,* ill-treated.

139   *heresies,* false beliefs. Men who turn away from the false doctrines they believed in, loathe those doctrines afterwards.

143   *address,* direct.

145–56   *Help . . . immediately.* What changes in speed of speaking, pitch of voice, and posture and movement are appropriate?

149   *Methought . . . away.* Emblematic of grief and despair. In Ripa's *Iconologia,* both emotions are represented by woodcuts of men with serpents gnawing at their breasts.

150   *prey,* devouring.

154   *of all loves,* in the name of everything that loves.

156   *Either death.* Helena also considers the possibility of death, II. i, 244. Is this exaggerated or real?

When at your hands did I deserve this scorn?
Is 't not enough, is 't not enough, young man,
That I did never, no nor never can,
Deserve a sweet look from Demetrius' eye,
But you must flout my insufficiency?
Good troth you do me wrong, good sooth you do,
In such disdainful manner me to woo.   130
But fare you well; perforce I must confess
I thought you lord of more true gentleness.
O, that a lady, of one man refused,
Should of another therefore be abused.   [*Exit*

LYSANDER: She sees not Hermia. Hermia, sleep thou there,
 And never mayst thou come Lysander near.
 For as a surfeit of the sweetest things
 The deepest loathing to the stomach brings;
 Or as the heresies that men do leave
 Are hated most of those they did deceive;   140
 So thou, my surfeit and my heresy,
 Of all be hated; but the most of me.
 And all my powers address your love and might,
 To honour Helen and to be her knight.   [*Exit*

HERMIA: [*Awaking*] Help me Lysander, help me; do thy best
 To pluck this crawling serpent from my breast.
 Ay me, for pity! What a dream was here!
 Lysander look how I do quake with fear.
 Methought a serpent eat my heart away,
 And you sat smiling at his cruel prey.   150
 Lysander! What, removed? Lysander, lord!
 What, out of hearing, gone? No sound, no word?
 Alack where are you? Speak, an if you hear.
 Speak, of all loves! I swoon almost with fear.
 No? Then I will perceive you are not nigh;
 Either death or you I'll find immediately.   [*Exit*

The wood

Do the 'mechanicals' arrive together, or in small groups from different entrances? Any lights required?

2   *Pat*, just right, promptly.

4   *tiring-house*, dressing room.

6   *Peter Quince.* Any action leading to this?
7   *bully*, good friend, fine.

12   *By'r lakin*, by Our Lady. *lakin*, ladykin, little lady. *parlous*, perilous.

16   *prologue* (second), speaker of the prologue. *seem to say*, see fit to say, say what amounts to.
     Bottom's device would destroy the whole dramatic illusion.
18–20 *tell . . . fear*. Unconscious irony.

21–2 *Well . . . six*. Is Quince eager or reluctant?
22   *eight and six*, i.e. syllables in alternate lines of verse. See Bottom's song, 'The ousel cock'.
23–4 *eight and eight*. See Hecate's speech in *Macbeth*, III. v. Is Bottom right, disagreeing on principle, asserting his superior judgement, thinking the longer the line the better the verse?

ACT THREE

SCENE ONE

TITANIA *lying asleep*

Enter QUINCE, SNUG, BOTTOM, FLUTE, SNOUT, *and* STARVELING

BOTTOM: Are we all met?

QUINCE: Pat, pat; and here's a marvellous convenient place for our rehearsal. This green plot shall be our stage, this hawthorn-brake our tiring-house, and we will do it in action, as we will do it before the duke.

BOTTOM: Peter Quince.

QUINCE: What sayest thou, bully Bottom?

BOTTOM: There are things in this comedy of Pyramus and Thisby that will never please. First, Pyramus must draw a sword to kill himself; which the ladies cannot abide. How answer you that?   11

SNOUT: By 'r lakin, a parlous fear.

STARVELING: I believe we must leave the killing out, when all is done.

BOTTOM: Not a whit, I have a device to make all well. Write me a prologue, and let the prologue seem to say, we will do no harm with our swords, and that Pyramus is not killed indeed. And, for the more better assurance, tell them that I Pyramus am not Pyramus, but Bottom the weaver; this will put them out of fear.   20

QUINCE: Well, we will have such a prologue, and it shall be written in eight and six.

BOTTOM: No, make it two more; let it be written in eight and eight.

25   *ladies . . . lion*, e.g. as Thisby in the play.

28   *God shield us*. Any gesture? *lion among ladies*. Possibly an allusion to an incident at the christening of Prince Henry of Scotland on 30th August, 1594. A triumphal car was to have been drawn by a lion, but lest the lion should frighten the spectators, or itself be disturbed by the lights a Moor was substituted. The phrase, however, following the proverb, 'A lion among sheep and a sheep among lions', could imply one who was only courageous in the presence of ladies.

29   *fearful wild-fowl*, (a) terrifying wild beast, (b) timid wild-fowl.

31   *another prologue*. Hardly therefore a prologue.

32–40 *Nay . . . joiner*. Again Bottom would destroy the dramatic illusion.

32   *you . . . name*, i.e. in the second prologue instead of saying he is not a lion.

34   *defect*, (a) effect, (b) unfortunate result.

35–6 *wish . . . entreat*. See I. ii, 83. Any gestures during this battering of the brain?

37–8 *it . . . life*, it would be the greatest pity.

38–40 *No . . . joiner*. It has been suggested that there is a reference here to an incident in the pageantry at Kenilworth during Elizabeth's visit (1575) mentioned in *Merry Passages and Jests*. Harry Goldingham playing the part of Arion on the Dolphin's back found his voice very hoarse. He 'teares off his disguise, and swears he was none of Arion, not he, but e'en honest Harry Goldingham; which blunt discoverie pleased the Queen better than if it had gone through in the right way'.

45   *A . . . almanac*. Almanacs were noted for containing foolish astrological forecasts.

46   *moonshine*, (a) moonlight, (b) foolish nonsense.
      Any movement? Who produces the calendar?

51–2 *bush . . . lanthorn*. The 'man in the moon' was so represented. According to legends he was Isaac with the wood for sacrifice, Cain with thorns the fruit of his wilderness offered for sacrifice, or the man stoned to death by the Israelites for gathering sticks on the sabbath (*Numbers*, xv. 32).

52   *disfigure*, figure, perform, display.

56   *You . . . wall*, Craik (*Tudor Interlude*) notes that the comedy rests on the fantastic circumvention by the mechanicals of the building of a stage wall, a thing they could quite easily do, particularly with the help of Snug, the joiner.

58   *loam*, clay. *rough-cast*, mixture of lime and gravel.

SNOUT: Will not the ladies be afeard of the lion?

STARVELING: I fear it, I promise you.

BOTTOM: Masters, you ought to consider with yourselves—to bring in, God shield us, a lion among ladies, is a most dreadful thing. For there is not a more fearful wild-fowl than your lion living; and we ought to look to 't. 30

SNOUT: Therefore another prologue must tell he is not a lion.

BOTTOM: Nay, you must name his name, and half his face must be seen through the lion's neck, and he himself must speak through, saying thus, or to the same defect: 'Ladies,' or, 'Fair ladies, I would wish you,' or, 'I would request you,' or, 'I would entreat you, not to fear, not to tremble; my life for yours. If you think I come hither as a lion, it were pity of my life. No, I am no such thing, I am a man as other men are;' and there indeed let him name his name, and tell them plainly he is Snug the joiner. 40

QUINCE: Well, it shall be so. But there is two hard things; that is, to bring the moonlight into a chamber; for you know, Pyramus and Thisby meet by moonlight.

SNOUT: Doth the moon shine that night we play our play?

BOTTOM: A calendar, a calendar, look in the almanac; find out moonshine, find out moonshine.

QUINCE: Yes, it doth shine that night.

BOTTOM: Why then may you leave a casement of the great chamber window, where we play, open, and the moon may shine in at the casement. 50

QUINCE: Ay, or else one must come in with a bush of thorns and a lanthorn, and say he comes to disfigure, or to present, the person of moonshine. Then, there is another thing: we must have a wall in the great chamber, for Pyramus and Thisby, says the story, did talk through the chink of a wall.

SNOUT: You can never bring in a wall. What say you Bottom?

BOTTOM: Some man or other must present wall: and let him have some plaster, or some loam, or some rough-cast about

63   *brake*, undergrowth, bushes.

65   *hempen home-spuns*, woolly nit-wits, numskulls in their home-mades. Hemp was formerly grown in England. *swaggering*. Perhaps Bottom is striking postures.

67   *toward*, about to begin.

70   *of*. Dover Wilson reads 'ha'' = have. *savours*. Sisson takes this as a verb in the plural.

79   *to . . . heard*. Another phrase made quaint by the omission of say, 'what it was that made the'.

80–4 *Most . . . tomb*. Is Flute's voice unbroken, falsetto, counter-tenor, or yodelling?

80–1 *radiant . . . rose*. Some contradictions in colouring, in any case the epithets would be better applied to Thisby.

82   *brisky juvenal*, smart young fellow, lively youngster. *Jew*. Dover Wilson suggests that this is a playful diminutive for 'juvenal'. Verity suggests that 'jewel' may be meant.

84   *Ninny's*, (*a*) fool's, (*b*) Ninus'.

85   *Ninus' tomb*. Ninus was the founder-king of Nineveh.

him, to signify wall; and let him hold his fingers thus, and
through that cranny shall Pyramus and Thisby whisper.   60
QUINCE: If that may be, then all is well. Come, sit down, every
mother's son, and rehearse your parts. Pyramus, you begin.
When you have spoken your speech, enter into that brake; and
so every one according to his cue.

Enter PUCK

PUCK: What hempen home-spuns have we swaggering here,
So near the cradle of the Fairy Queen?
What, a play toward! I'll be an auditor,
An actor too perhaps, if I see cause.
QUINCE: Speak, Pyramus. Thisby stand forth.
BOTTOM: Thisby, the flowers of odious savours sweet—   70
QUINCE: Odours, odours.
BOTTOM: ——odours savours sweet,
So hath thy breath, my dearest Thisby dear.
But hark, a voice; stay thou but here awhile,
And by and by I will to thee appear.   [*Exit*
PUCK: A stranger Pyramus than e'er played here.   [*Exit*
FLUTE: Must I speak now?
QUINCE: Ay marry, must you. For you must understand he goes
but to see a noise that he heard, and is to come again.
FLUTE: Most radiant Pyramus, most lily-white of hue,   80
Of colour like the red rose on triumphant briar,
Most brisky juvenal, and eke most lovely Jew,
As true as truest horse, that yet would never tire,
I'll meet thee Pyramus, at Ninny's tomb.
QUINCE: 'Ninus' tomb', man. Why you must not speak that
yet; that you answer to Pyramus. You speak all your part at
once, cues and all. Pyramus enter, your cue is past; it is, 'never
tire.'
FLUTE: O—As true as truest horse, that yet would never tire.

90   *If . . . thine*. Bottom, like Quince later, misreads his part with apt
       results. Dover Wilson suggests that the line was 'If I were (i.e.
       true), fair Thisby, I were only thine'.

93–7   *I'll . . . burn*. Should Puck deliver this speech from the front of the
       stage as an aside to the audience, should he be driving off or teasing
       individual 'mechanicals', should he mimic in any way the trans-
       formations he names?
95–8   *Sometime . . . turn*. Popular belief credited Puck with such changes
       of shape.

104   *translated*, transformed.

109   *ousel cock*. Here the cock-blackbird.

112   *little quill*, i.e. shrill, small pipe.
113–   *What . . . thee*. Compare Demetrius' speech, III. ii, 137 ff., and
   25 Lysander's, II. ii, 103 ff.

116   *plain-song*, simple, unvarying song.

Enter PUCK, *and* BOTTOM *with an ass's head*

BOTTOM: If I were fair, Thisby, I were only thine.   90
QUINCE: O monstrous! O strange! We are haunted. Pray
   masters fly, masters! Help!
             [Exeunt Quince, Snug, Flute, Snout, and Starveling
PUCK: I'll follow you, I'll lead you about a round,
   Through bog, through bush, through brake, through briar.
   Sometime a horse I'll be, sometime a hound,
    A hog, a headless bear, sometime a fire,
   And neigh, and bark, and grunt, and roar, and burn,
   Like horse, hound, hog, bear, fire, at every turn.   *[Exit*
BOTTOM: Why do they run away? This is a knavery of them to
   make me afeard.   100

Enter SNOUT

SNOUT: O Bottom, thou art changed. What do I see on thee?
BOTTOM: What do you see? You see an ass-head of your own,
   do you?   *[Exit Snout*

Enter QUINCE

QUINCE: Bless thee Bottom, bless thee. Thou art translated.
                          [Exit
BOTTOM: I see their knavery. This is to make an ass of me, to
   fright me, if they could. But I will not stir from this place, do
   what they can. I will walk up and down here, and I will sing,
   that they shall hear I am not afraid.   *[Sings*
       The ousel cock so black of hue,
         With orange-tawny bill,   110
       The throstle with his note so true,
         The wren with little quill—
TITANIA: *[Awaking]* What angel wakes me from my flowery
   bed?
BOTTOM: *[Sings]*
       The finch, the sparrow, and the lark,
         The plain-song cuckoo grey,

118   *nay*, i.e. refuse to believe the implication of a cry 'cuckoo', that his
      wife was unfaithful. Bottom pronounces it 'neigh' in donkey-
      fashion.

119   *set his wit*, pit his wits against, bother to challenge.

120   *never so*, without ceasing.

121–5 *I ... thee*. Has Titania risen? What gestures or movements are
      appropriate?

123–5 *So ... thee*, i.e. in the platonic view Bottom's outward beauty,
      reflects his inner virtue.

123   *enthralled to*, captivated by.

124   *fair virtue's force*, the influence of your manly qualities.

127–8 *reason ... now-a-days*. An apt comment on the four lovers and on
      Titania.

130   *gleek*, make a sharp comment.

131   *Thou ... beautiful*. Further platonic argument, its irony capped by
      Bottom's disclaimer.

134   *Out ... go*. What is the intention of the rhyme here and in ll.
      147–56, 175–9—to stress the emotion, intensify the wooing,
      emphasize the descriptive passages or the delights of fairyland?

137   *The ... state*, it is always summer where I am. Perhaps an allusion
      to the Summer Lady, or Queen, of the May games.

142   *purge*, cleanse, purify.

s.D. *Peaseblossom ... Mustardseed*. How do the fairies appear—
      through trap-doors or normal entrances, in order of speaking, as a
      group, swiftly?
          Should they carry tapers here and II. ii? See ll. 151–3.

Whose note full many a man doth mark,
And dares not answer, nay—

for indeed, who would set his wit to so foolish a bird? Who
would give a bird the lie, though he cry 'cuckoo' never so? 120

TITANIA: I pray thee, gentle mortal, sing again.
Mine ear is much enamoured of thy note;
So is mine eye enthralled to thy shape,
And thy fair virtue's force perforce doth move me,
On the first view to say, to swear, I love thee.

BOTTOM: Methinks mistress, you should have little reason for
that. And yet, to say the truth, reason and love keep little
company together now-a-days. The more the pity that some
honest neighbours will not make them friends. Nay, I can
gleek upon occasion. 130

TITANIA: Thou art as wise as thou art beautiful.

BOTTOM: Not so neither. But if I had wit enough to get out of
this wood, I have enough to serve mine own turn

TITANIA: Out of this wood do not desire to go.
Thou shalt remain here, whether thou wilt or no.
I am a spirit of no common rate.
The summer still doth tend upon my state,
And I do love thee; therefore, go with me
I'll give thee fairies to attend on thee;
And they shall fetch thee jewels from the deep, 140
And sing, while thou on pressed flowers dost sleep.
And I will purge thy mortal grossness so,
That thou shalt like an airy spirit go.
Peaseblossom, Cobweb, Moth, and Mustardseed!

Enter PEASEBLOSSOM, COBWEB, MOTH, *and*
MUSTARDSEED

PEASEBLOSSOM: Ready.
COBWEB: And I.
MOTH: And I.

148   *dewberries*, blackberries with large drupes, but the word was sometimes used of gooseberries in Shakespeare's time.

154   *painted*, brightly coloured.

157   *Hail*. What 'courtesies' are appropriate?
158   *cry . . . mercy*, beg pardon. *worships*. Bottom is also courteous—over courteous.

      Bottom strives to produce elegant, courtly phrases, but his subject matter remains homely.

162   *If . . . you*. Cobwebs were placed on wounds to stop bleeding.

165–6 *Mistress . . . father*. Perhaps some unconscious humour by Bottom, who confuses 'peascod' with 'codpiece', an appendage to breeches, and hence essentially male.
165   *Squash*, unripe pea-pod.

172   *house*, family.

MUSTARDSEED: And I.

ALL: Where shall we go?

TITANIA: Be kind and courteous to this gentleman,
 Hop in his walks and gambol in his eyes,
 Feed him with apricocks and dewberries,
 With purple grapes, green figs, and mulberries.
 The honey-bags steal from the humble-bees,   150
 And for night-tapers crop their waxen thighs,
 And light them at the fiery glow-worm's eyes,
 To have my love to bed and to arise;
 And pluck the wings from painted butterflies,
 To fan the moonbeams from his sleeping eyes.
 Nod to him elves, and do him courtesies.

PEASEBLOSSOM: Hail, mortal!

COBWEB: Hail!

MOTH: Hail!

MUSTARDSEED: Hail!

BOTTOM: I cry your worships mercy heartily. I beseech your worship's name.

COBWEB: Cobweb.   160

BOTTOM: I shall desire you of more acquaintance, good Master Cobweb. If I cut my finger, I shall make bold with you. Your name honest gentleman?

PEASEBLOSSOM: Peaseblossom.

BOTTOM: I pray you commend me to Mistress Squash your mother, and to Master Peascod your father. Good Master Peaseblossom, I shall desire you of more acquaintance too. Your name I beseech you sir?

MUSTARDSEED: Mustardseed.   169

BOTTOM: Good Master Mustardseed, I know your patience well. That same cowardly, giant-like ox-beef hath devoured many a gentleman of your house. I promise you your kindred hath made my eyes water ere now. I desire you of more acquaintance, good Master Mustardseed.

178   *enforced*, violated.

179   *Tie . . . silently*. Is Bottom braying too much? However, silence was traditionally necessary to enter fairyland. How should the fairies carry out this instruction? Is Titania impatient that Bottom is not showing her attention so that Moth is not introduced?

The wood

Oberon's entry should perhaps be formal with stylized movements.

2   *next*, nearest.

3   *in extremity*, desperately.

4   *mad*. How should Puck's entry justify this description? Why is he 'mad' at this point?

5   *night-rule*, order of things by night. *haunted*. Perhaps an echo of Quince's 'haunted', III. i, 91.

7   *close*, secret.

8   *dull*, drowsy.

9   *crew of patches*, band of stupid fellows. *rude*, rough.

13   *shallowest thick-skin*, lightest-brained blockhead. Men were considered the nearer to beasts the thicker their skin was. *barren sort*, brainless set.

17   *nole*, noddle, head. Any demonstration of the change?

19   *mimic*, actor.

21   *russet-pated choughs*, grey-headed jackdaws. *sort*, flock.

TITANIA: Come wait upon, lead him to my bower.
    The moon methinks looks with a watery eye,
And when she weeps, weeps every little flower,
    Lamenting some enforced chastity.
Tie up my love's tongue, bring him silently.   *[Exeunt*

SCENE TWO

Enter OBERON

OBERON: I wonder if Titania be awaked;
    Then, what it was that next came in her eye,
    Which she must dote on in extremity.

Enter PUCK

    Here comes my messenger. How now, mad spirit?
    What night-rule now about this haunted grove?
PUCK: My mistress with a monster is in love.
    Near to her close and consecrated bower,
    While she was in her dull and sleeping hour,
    A crew of patches, rude mechanicals,
    That work for bread upon Athenian stalls,   10
    Were met together to rehearse a play
    Intended for great Theseus' nuptial day.
    The shallowest thick-skin of that barren sort,
    Who Pyramus presented, in their sport
    Forsook his scene and entered in a brake,
    When I did him at this advantage take.
    An ass's nole I fixed on his head.
    Anon his Thisby must be answered,
    And forth my mimic comes. When they him spy,
    As wild geese that the creeping fowler eye,   20
    Or russet-pated choughs, many in sort,
    Rising and cawing at the gun's report,

24   *his sight*, i.e. sight of him.
25   *at our stamp*. The Quarto reading. Some editors prefer Johnson's emendation 'at a stump'. For the idea of stamping see IV. i, 83.

27   *sense*, i.e. senses.
28   *senseless*. A quibble with 'sense . . . lost', l. 27.

36   *latched*, moistened.

s.**D.**   Who enters first?
41   *Stand close*, hide, keep out of sight.
44   *Lay . . . bitter*, inflict so bitter a speech. 'Lay on' implies a curse. See l. 46 where Hermia by emphasizing 'hast given' plays upon this meaning.
45   *should*, ought to.
48   *o'er . . . deep*. See Macbeth, III. iv, 136–8; *Richard III*, IV. ii, 65–6 for similar thought. *o'er . . . blood*, i.e. taken the first step in shedding blood.
52–5   *I'll . . . Antipodes*. This image extends the thought expressed in l. 50. It also reflects the theme of disorder through female dominance.
52   *Hermia*. What effect is gained by this reference to herself by name?
53   *whole*, intact, unpierced.
54   *displease*, upset. Perhaps a quibble on 'displace'. Is this another hint of female unruliness?
55   *her brother's*. In classical myth Phoebe, the moon goddess was the sister of Phoebus Apollo, the sun-god. *Antipodes*, the inhabitants of the southern hemisphere.

Sever themselves, and madly sweep the sky,
So, at his sight, away his fellows fly;
And, at our stamp, here o'er and o'er one falls;
He 'murder' cries and help from Athens calls.
Their sense thus weak, lost with their fears thus strong,
Made senseless things begin to do them wrong.
For briars and thorns at their apparel snatch,
Some sleeves, some hats; from yielders all things catch.   30
I led them on in this distracted fear,
And left sweet Pyramus translated there.
When in that moment, so it came to pass,
Titania waked and straightway loved an ass.
OBERON: This falls out better than I could devise,
But hast thou yet latched the Athenian's eyes
With the love-juice, as I did bid thee do?
PUCK: I took him sleeping—that is finished too—
And the Athenian woman by his side;
That when he waked, of force she must be eyed.   40

Enter HERMIA *and* DEMETRIUS

OBERON: Stand close, this is the same Athenian.
PUCK: This is the woman, but not this the man.
DEMETRIUS: O why rebuke you him that loves you so?
Lay breath so bitter on your bitter foe.
HERMIA: Now I but chide, but I should use thee worse,
For thou, I fear, has given me cause to curse.
If thou has slain Lysander in his sleep,
Being o'er shoes in blood, plunge in the deep,
And kill me too.
The sun was not so true unto the day   50
As he to me. Would he have stolen away
From sleeping Hermia? I'll believe as soon
This whole earth may be bored, and that the moon
May through the centre creep, and so displease
Her brother's noontide with th' Antipodes.

63   *give him me*, i.e. his body.

64   *carcass*. The word deepens Hermia's fears, and she jumps to a false
conclusion.

67   *Henceforth . . . men*, i.e. you are now a beast—a cur.

68   *O . . . sake*. Any gestures or movements to mark the alternation of
pleading and cursing?

70   *touch*, (*a*) deed, (*b*) dishonour.

71   *worm*, snake.

72   *doubler tongue*, i.e. a more treacherous weapon.

74   *misprised mood*, feelings roused by a mistake.

77   *I . . . well*. Hermia requires positive assurance.

79   *privilege*, (*a*) a right to some advantage, (*b*) an immunity from
doing something. The two senses are blended by a kind of quibble
in this sentence.

80–1   *And . . . no*. Is Hermia furious, hysterical, raging, supercilious,
contemptuous, savage?

82   *vein*, mood.

87   *for his tender*, for sleep's offer of payment.

It cannot be but thou hast murdered him.
So should a murderer look; so dead, so grim.
DEMETRIUS: So should the murdered look, and so should I,
Pierced through the heart with your stern cruelty.
Yet you, the murderer, look as bright, as clear,   60
As yonder Venus in her glimmering sphere.
HERMIA: What's this to my Lysander? Where is he?
Ah good Demetrius, wilt thou give him me?
DEMETRIUS: I had rather give his carcass to my hounds.
HERMIA: Out dog, out cur! Thou drivest me past the bounds
Of maiden's patience. Hast thou slain him then?
Henceforth be never numbered among men.
O, once tell true; tell true, even for my sake.
Durst thou have looked upon him being awake?
And hast thou killed him sleeping? O brave touch.   70
Could not a worm, an adder, do so much?
An adder did it; for with doubler tongue
Than thine, thou serpent, never adder stung.
DEMETRIUS: You spend your passion on a misprised mood.
I am not guilty of Lysander's blood;
Nor is he dead, for aught that I can tell.
HERMIA: I pray thee, tell me then that he is well.
DEMETRIUS: An if I could, what should I get therefore?
HERMIA: A privilege never to see me more.
And from thy hated presence part I so.   80
See me no more, whether he be dead or no.   [*Exit*
DEMETRIUS: There is no following her in this fierce vein.
Here therefore for a while I will remain.
So sorrow's heaviness doth heavier grow
For debt that bankrupt sleep doth sorrow owe;
Which now in some slight measure it will pay,
If for his tender here I make some stay.

                          [*Lies down and sleeps*
OBERON: What hast thou done? Thou hast mistaken quite,

90 *misprision*, mistake.

91 *turned*, i.e. turned false. *false*. How does Oberon know Demetrius' falseness?

92-3 *fate . . . fail*, fate's law that for every man that is true in love a million are not.

93 *confounding . . . oath*, breaking their promises time and time again.

96 *fancy-sick*, love-sick. *cheer*, face.

97 *sighs . . . dear*. It was believed that every sigh drew a drop of blood from the heart. See *2 Henry VI*, III. ii, 61.

99 *against*, in readiness for.

100-1 *I . . . bow*. What movement would be appropriate—headlong, bounding, tripping, leaping?

101 *Tartar's bow*. The Tartar tribes from the east of the Caspian Sea were famous for their light-armed, mounted bowmen.

104 *apple*, pupil.

113 *lover's fee*. Supposed to be three kisses.

114 *fond pageant*, foolish spectacle, silly performance. Puck points out the proper attitude for the audience to adopt.

119 *alone*, unequalled.

And laid the love-juice on some true-love's sight.
Of thy misprision must perforce ensue   90
Some true love turned, and not a false turned true.
PUCK: Then fate o'er-rules, that one man holding troth,
  A million fail, confounding oath on oath.
OBERON: About the wood go swifter than the wind,
  And Helena of Athens look thou find.
  All fancy-sick she is and pale of cheer,
  With sighs of love, that costs the fresh blood dear:
  By some illusion see thou bring her here.
  I'll charm his eyes against she do appear.
PUCK: I go, I go, look how I go,   100
  Swifter than arrow from the Tartar's bow.   [*Exit*
OBERON: Flower of this purple dye,
       Hit with Cupid's archery,
       Sink in apple of his eye.
       When his love he doth espy,
       Let her shine as gloriously
       As the Venus of the sky.
       When thou wakest, if she be by,
       Beg of her for remedy.

Enter PUCK
PUCK: Captain of our fairy band,   110
       Helena is here at hand,
       And the youth, mistook by me,
       Pleading for a lover's fee.
       Shall we their fond pageant see?
       Lord, what fools these mortals be!
OBERON: Stand aside. The noise they make
       Will cause Demetrius to awake.
PUCK: Then will two at once woo one,
       That must needs be sport alone.
       And those things do best please me   120

121   *preposterously*, topsy turvily.

122–7   *Why . . . true.* A six-lined verse. See Helena's reply ll. 128–33 and ll. 431–6; 442–7.

124–7   *when . . . true.* Perhaps two thoughts underlie this argument (*a*) the mother's grief at the pain of birth, (*b*) the repentance and vows at baptism, both matters of christian faith. See *Genesis*, iii. 16 and *St. John*, iii. 5, *St. Mark*, i. 4.

127   *badge of faith*, i.e. (*a*) his tears, (*b*) Christian faith.

129   *O devilish-holy fray.* i.e. like the Devil you are using scriptural authority to gain your own ends. Helena scornfully sums up Lysander's fanciful pleading with its christian allusion in a forceful oxymoron.

131–3   *you . . . tales*, i.e. there is no substance in your vows either to me or to Hermia.

133   *light*, (*a*) false, (*b*) lightweight. *tales*, (*a*) idle talk, i.e. breath, (*b*) falsehoods.

136   *Demetrius . . . you.* A nicely timed cue for Demetrius to awake.

137   *nymph*, i.e. goddess.

141   *congealed*, frozen. *Taurus'*. A mountain range in south Turkey.

142   *turns . . . crow*, is as black as a crow by comparison.

144   *princess . . . white*, supreme (sovereign) whiteness. *seal*, i.e. her hand which can seal a pledge. Perhaps there is a glance at the sense of 'hand in marriage', and hence 'pledge' or 'symbol'.

That befall preposterously.

Enter LYSANDER *and* HELENA

LYSANDER: Why should you think that I should woo in scorn?
    Scorn and derision never come in tears.
  Look when I vow, I weep; and vows so born,
    In their nativity all truth appears.
  How can these things in me seem scorn to you,
  Bearing the badge of faith to prove them true?
HELENA: You do advance your cunning more and more.
    When truth kills truth, O devilish-holy fray!
  These vows are Hermia's. Will you give her o'er?   130
    Weigh oath with oath, and you will nothing weigh.
  Your vows to her and me, put in two scales,
  Will even weigh, and both as light as tales.
LYSANDER: I had no judgement when to her I swore.
HELENA: Nor none, in my mind, now you give her o'er.
LYSANDER: Demetrius loves her, and he loves not you.
DEMETRIUS: [*Awaking*] O Helen, goddess, nymph, perfect, divine!
  To what, my love, shall I compare thine eyne?
  Crystal is muddy. O, how ripe in show
  Thy lips, those kissing cherries, tempting grow!   140
  That pure congealed white, high Taurus' snow,
  Fanned with the eastern wind, turns to a crow
  When thou hold'st up thy hand. O let me kiss
  This princess of pure white, this seal of bliss.
HELENA: O spite! O hell! I see you all are bent
  To set against me for your merriment.
  If you were civil and knew courtesy,
  You would not do me thus much injury.
  Can you not hate me, as I know you do,
  But you must join in souls to mock me too?   150
  If you were men, as men you are in show,

157   *trim*, fine. Ironic.

158   *conjure*, raise. Perhaps a quibble on the original meaning of the word, 'swear together', which aptly recalls the oaths sworn by both men (l. 153).

160   *extort*, tear away.

161   *A . . . sport.* Helena moves away in tears leaving the two men together. Is she angry, sorrowful, ridiculous, pitiful, impatient?

171   *sojourned*, stayed for a short time.

172   *And . . . returned.* Proverbially the lover's home was regarded as the lady's breast. See Sonnet 109.

175   *aby*, pay for.

180   *pays.* Perhaps an echo of 'impair'.

You would not use a gentle lady so;
To vow, and swear, and superpraise my parts,
When I am sure you hate me with your hearts.
You both are rivals, and love Hermia;
And now both rivals, to mock Helena.
A trim exploit, a manly enterprise,
To conjure tears up in a poor maid's eyes
With your derision. None of noble sort
Would so offend a virgin, and extort   160
A poor soul's patience, all to make you sport.
LYSANDER: You are unkind, Demetrius; be not so,
For you love Hermia; this you know I know.
And here, with all good will, with all my heart,
In Hermia's love I yield you up my part;
And yours of Helena to me bequeath,
Whom I do love, and will do till my death.
HELENA: Never did mockers waste more idle breath.
DEMETRIUS: Lysander, keep thy Hermia; I will none.
If e'er I loved her, all that love is gone.   170
My heart to her but as guest-wise sojourned,
And now to Helen is it home returned,
There to remain.
LYSANDER: Helen, it is not so.
DEMETRIUS: Disparage not the faith thou dost not know,
Lest to thy peril thou aby it dear.
Look where thy love comes; yonder is thy dear.
                    Enter HERMIA
HERMIA: Dark night, that from the eye his function takes,
The ear more quick of apprehension makes.
Wherein it doth impair the seeing sense,
It pays the hearing double recompense.   180
Thou art not by mine eye, Lysander, found;
Mine ear, I thank it, brought me to thy sound.
But why unkindly didst thou leave me so?

185   *press Lysander from.* Emphatic as the opposite of what might be expected.

187–8 *Helena . . . light.* Perhaps a glance at the meaning of the word Helena—meteor, torch.

188   *oes,* circles. *eyes,* stars.

189– *Why . . . so?* Any movement or gesture?
90

191   *You . . . be.* Is Hermia stunned, shocked, or under the belief that Lysander is pretending or deluded?

194   *false . . . me,* deceitful game to spite me.

195 ff. Does the change to blank verse mark—a passage of narrative, an alteration to the text, a change of subject or mood?

195   *Injurious,* wilfully inflicting wrong on another.

197   *bait,* harass, attack.

198   *counsel,* secrets.

200–1 *When . . . us,* i.e. the time spent together passed so quickly.

203   *artificial gods,* gods who create things made by art.

208   *incorporate,* belonging to one body.

210   *union in partition.* Perfect friendship was characterized by identity of soul or heart between the friends, 'one soul in bodies twain'.

213   *Two . . . first,* i.e. bodies.

213– *like . . . crest,* like the two separate coats of arms of a man and his
  14 wife are combined to form one coat surmounted by a single crest.

       Friendship at its highest between man and man was regarded by some as superior to the love between a man and woman. Friendship between women was unusual but was also very highly esteemed. The passionate description of the ideal friendship existing between Hermia and Helena sharpens the contrast of their present predicament.

LYSANDER: Why should he stay, whom love doth press to go?
HERMIA: What love could press Lysander from my side?
LYSANDER: Lysander's love, that would not let him bide,
  Fair Helena, who more engilds the night
  Than all yon fiery oes and eyes of light.
  Why seek'st thou me? Could not this make thee know,
  The hate I bear thee made me leave thee so?   190
HERMIA: You speak not as you think; it cannot be.
HELENA: Lo, she is one of this confederacy.
  Now I perceive they have conjoined all three
  To fashion this false sport in spite of me.
  Injurious Hermia, most ungrateful maid,
  Have you conspired, have you with these contrived
  To bait me with this foul derision?
  Is all the counsel that we two have shared,
  The sisters' vows, the hours that we have spent,
  When we have chid the hasty-footed time   200
  For parting us—O, is all forgot?
  All school-days' friendship, childhood innocence?
  We, Hermia, like two artificial gods,
  Have with our needles created both one flower,
  Both on one sampler, sitting on one cushion,
  Both warbling of one song, both in one key,
  As if our hands, our sides, voices, and minds
  Had been incorporate. So we grew together,
  Like to a double cherry, seeming parted,
  But yet an union in partition,   210
  Two lovely berries moulded on one stem.
  So with two seeming bodies, but one heart,
  Two of the first, like coats in heraldry,
  Due but to one, and crowned with one crest.
  And will you rent our ancient love asunder,
  To join with men in scorning your poor friend?
  It is not friendly, 't is not maidenly.

237   *persever*. Accented on the second syllable. *counterfeit sad looks*, i.e. because they are inwardly laughing.

238–9 *Make . . . other*. Perhaps attempts by the other three to communicate with each other in their bewilderment prompt this outburst.

239   *sweet*. Sarcastic.

240   *carried*, maintained. *chronicled*, set down on record.

242   *argument*, subject for joking.

245–   *Stay . . . Helena*. The pace quickens in these lines which are
81   accompanied by movement, struggling, and gestures.

    Our sex, as well as I, may chide you for it,
    Though I alone do feel the injury.
HERMIA: I am amazed at your passionate words.   **220**
    I scorn you not. It seems that you scorn me.
HELENA: Have you not set Lysander, as in scorn,
    To follow me and praise my eyes and face?
    And made your other love, Demetrius,
    Who even but now did spurn me with his foot,
    To call me goddess, nymph, divine, and rare,
    Precious, celestial? Wherefore speaks he this
    To her he hates? And wherefore doth Lysander
    Deny your love, so rich within his soul,
    And tender me, forsooth, affection,   **230**
    But by your setting on, by your consent?
    What though I be not so in grace as you,
    So hung upon with love, so fortunate,
    But miserable most, to love unloved?
    This you should pity rather than despise.
HERMIA: I understand not what you mean by this.
HELENA: Ay, do, persever, counterfeit sad looks.
    Make mouths upon me when I turn my back.
    Wink each at other, hold the sweet jest up.
    This sport well carried, shall be chronicled.   **240**
    If you have any pity, grace, or manners,
    You would not make me such an argument.
    But fare ye well, 't is partly my own fault,
    Which death or absence soon shall remedy.
LYSANDER: Stay gentle Helena, hear my excuse;
    My love, my life, my soul, fair Helena.
HELENA: O excellent!
HERMIA: Sweet, do not scorn her so.
DEMETRIUS: If she cannot entreat, I can compel.
LYSANDER: Thou canst compel no more than she entreat.
    Thy threats have no more strength than her weak prayers. **250**

256   *Lysander . . . this.* Hermia realizes that the two are about to fight and clings to Lysander.

257   *you Ethiop*, you black creature. Dark beauty was unfashionable in the reign of the reddish-haired Elizabeth. *No, no, he'll.* Demetrius is heavily sarcastic at Lysander's attempts to free himself from Hermia. Some editors prefer the Folio reading 'No, no, Sir'.

258   *Take on*, put on a show of anger.

259   *tame*, cowardly.

262   *rude*, rough, ill-mannered.

263   *tawny Tartar*, swarthy barbarian.

264   *loathed . . . potion*. Perhaps a suggestion that Hermia had acted on him like a drug or love potion. If so, it is an ironic comment in view of the potion on his eyes.

267   *bond*, word on oath. Demetrius jeeringly suggests that even a very weak bond (Hermia's arms) manages to hold Lysander.

272   *what news*, what does this mean?

275   *Since*, during.

276–7   *Why . . . say?* What action is appropriate to this realization of the frightening truth?

279–   *Therefore . . . Helena*. How does Hermia respond to this—a pause,
81   a slow turn to Helena, a quick flare of temper, slow deliberate or rapid vicious speech?

Helen, I love thee, by my life I do.
I swear by that which I will lose for thee,
To prove him false that says I love thee not.

DEMETRIUS: I say I love thee more than he can do.

LYSANDER: If thou say so, withdraw, and prove it too.

DEMETRIUS: Quick, come—

HERMIA: Lysander, whereto tends all this?

LYSANDER: Away, you Ethiop!

DEMETRIUS: No, no; he'll
Seem to break loose. Take on as you would follow,
But yet come not. You are a tame man, go!

LYSANDER: Hang off thou cat, thou burr! Vile thing let loose,
Or I will shake thee from me like a serpent.   261

HERMIA: Why are you grown so rude? What change is this,
Sweet love?

LYSANDER: Thy love? Out tawny Tartar, out!
Out, loathed medicine! O hated potion, hence!

HERMIA: Do you not jest?

HELENA: Yes sooth, and so do you.

LYSANDER: Demetrius, I will keep my word with thee.

DEMETRIUS: I would I had your bond, for I perceive
A weak bond holds you. I'll not trust your word

LYSANDER: What, should I hurt her, strike her, kill her dead?
Although I hate her, I'll not harm her so.   270

HERMIA: What, can you do me greater harm than hate?
Hate me, wherefore? O me, what news, my love?
Am not I Hermia? Are not you Lysander?
I am as fair now as I was erewhile.
Since night you loved me; yet since night you left me.
Why then you left me—O, the gods forbid—
In earnest, shall I say?

LYSANDER: Ay, by my life.
And never did desire to see thee more.
Therefore be out of hope, of question, of doubt.

282 *juggler*, deceiver. *canker-blossom*, (*a*) a maggot eating the heart of a rose bud (see II. ii, 3), (*b*) a dog-rose flowering uselessly but which is wantonly provocative (see Sonnet 54).

288 *counterfeit*, play-acting cheat. *puppet*, (*a*) dwarf, (*b*) despicable actress, i.e. in playing a part according as the plot of the three would have the strings pulled.

292 *tall personage*. A mocking over emphasis. 'Personage' was associated with dignity and importance.
293 *prevailed with him*, succeeded in gaining his love.

300 *curst*, bad-tempered.
301 *shrewishness*, quarrelsomeness.
302 *right*, true, proper.

Be certain, nothing truer; 't is no jest 280
That I do hate thee and love Helena.

HERMIA: O me, you juggler, you canker-blossom,
You thief of love. What, have you come by night
And stolen my love's heart from him?

HELENA: Fine, i' faith!
Have you no modesty, no maiden shame,
No touch of bashfulness? What, will you tear
Impatient answers from my gentle tongue?
Fie, fie, you counterfeit, you puppet, you!

HERMIA: Puppet? Why so? Ay, that way goes the game.
Now I perceive that she hath made compare 290
Between our statures, she hath urged her height,
And with her personage, her tall personage,
Her height, forsooth, she hath prevailed with him.
And are you grown so high in his esteem,
Because I am so dwarfish and so low?
How low am I, thou painted maypole? Speak;
How low am I? I am not yet so low,
But that my nails can reach unto thine eyes.

HELENA: I pray you, though you mock me, gentlemen,
Let her not hurt me. I was never curst. 300
I have no gift at all in shrewishness.
I am a right maid for my cowardice.
Let her not strike me. You perhaps may think,
Because she is something lower than myself.
That I can match her.

HERMIA: Lower? Hark, again.

HELENA: Good Hermia, do not be so bitter with me.
I evermore did love you Hermia,
Did ever keep your counsels, never wronged you;
Save that, in love unto Demetrius,
I told him of your stealth unto this wood. 310
He followed you; for love I followed him.

316   *Let me go*, i.e. do not follow me.

321   *Be . . . Helena.* Is Hermia threatening Helena?

323–5 *O . . . fierce.* Is Helena fearful or a spiteful tell-tale?
323   *keen*, sharp, harsh.

327   *flout*, mock.

329   *minimus*, minute creature. *knot-grass*, (*a*) clung to and stifled the
       growth of other plants, (*b*) a decoction of it was believed to stunt
       human growth.
330   *bead*, (*a*) small ornament, (*b*) that which hangs round the neck.

338   *cheek by jowl*, side by side, neck and neck.
       The intention of Lysander and Demetrius is serious enough. Are
       they to be shown as ridiculous or not? Do they march out side by
       side in step and with similar posture, or do they come together at
       the exit?
339   *coil*, trouble. *'long of*, because of.

But he hath chid me hence and threatened me
To strike me, spurn me; nay, to kill me too.
And now, so you will let me quiet go,
To Athens will I bear my folly back,
And follow you no further. Let me go.
You see how simple and how fond I am.

HERMIA: Why, get you gone. Who is 't that hinders you?

HELENA: A foolish heart, that I leave here behind.

HERMIA: What with Lysander?

HELENA: With Demetrius.   320

LYSANDER: Be not afraid; she shall not harm thee Helena.

DEMETRIUS: No sir, she shall not, though you take her part.

HELENA: O, when she's angry, she is keen and shrewd.
She was a vixen when she went to school;
And though she be but little, she is fierce.

HERMIA: 'Little' again? Nothing but 'low' and 'little'.
Why will you suffer her to flout me thus?
Let me come to her.

LYSANDER: Get you gone, you dwarf,
You minimus, of hindering knot-grass made,
You bead, you acorn.

DEMETRIUS: You are too officious   330
In her behalf that scorns your services.
Let her alone; speak not of Helena;
Take not her part. For, if thou dost intend
Never so little show of love to her,
Thou shalt aby it.

LYSANDER: Now she holds me not.
Now follow, if thou dar'est, to try whose right,
Of thine or mine, is most in Helena.

DEMETRIUS: Follow? Nay, I'll go with thee, cheek by jowl.

                              [*Exeunt Lysander and Demetrius*

HERMIA: You, mistress, all this coil is 'long of you.
Nay, go not back.

340-4 *I . . . say*. What is the point of these rhymes?

345 *still*, always, constantly.

347 *shadows*, (*a*) fairies, (*b*) darkness.

352 *sort*, happen.

355 *Hie*, hurry.
356 *welkin*, heavens. *anon*, straightway.
357 *Acheron*, the underworld, hell. In classical myth a river of the underworld.

360 *tongue*, voice.
361 *wrong*, insults.

364 *death-counterfeiting sleep*. A frequent image in Shakespeare's plays.

367 *virtuous property*, quality, power.
368 *his might*, its power.
369 *wonted*, accustomed.

373 *league*, agreement, friendship. *date*, duration term.

HELENA: I will not trust you, I, 340
  Nor longer stay in your curst company.
  Your hands than mine are quicker for a fray,
  My legs are longer though, to run away.   [*Exit*
HERMIA: I am amazed, and know not what to say.   [*Exit*
OBERON: This is thy negligence. Still thou mistak'st,
  Or else committ'st thy knaveries wilfully.
PUCK: Believe me, king of shadows, I mistook.
  Did not you tell me I should know the man
  By the Athenian garments he had on?
  And so far blameless proves my enterprise, 350
  That I have 'nointed an Athenian's eyes;
  And so far am I glad it so did sort,
  As this their jangling I esteem a sport.
OBERON: Thou see'st these lovers seek a place to fight:
  Hie therefore Robin, overcast the night,
  The starry welkin cover thou anon
  With drooping fog as black as Acheron,
  And lead these testy rivals so astray,
  As one come not within another's way.
  Like to Lysander sometime frame thy tongue, 360
  Then stir Demetrius up with bitter wrong;
  And sometime rail thou like Demetrius;
  And from each other look thou lead them thus,
  Till o'er their brows death-counterfeiting sleep
  With leaden legs and batty wings doth creep.
  Then crush this herb into Lysander's eye,
  Whose liquor hath this virtuous property,
  To take from thence all error with his might,
  And make his eyeballs roll with wonted sight.
  When they next wake, all this derision 370
  Shall seem a dream and fruitless vision,
  And back to Athens shall the lovers wend,
  With league whose date till death shall never end.

379   *night's swift dragons.* In classical myth they drew the Chariot of
       Night.
380   *Aurora's harbinger*, herald of the morning, i.e. the planet Venus.

382–5 *damned . . . upon.* The ghosts of suicides who were buried at cross-
       roads or who drowned themselves were condemned to wander.
       Puck states that their shame kept them from wandering in day-
       light, though a more usual view was that they were punished if
       they lingered after cockcrow or dawn.

388   *But . . . sort.* Oberon disclaims any connexion with ghosts.
389   *I . . . sport*, (a) I have made merry with Aurora, or, (b) I have
       hunted with Cephalus, her lover. See V. i, 197.
389–   *I . . . streams.* Is this alchemy of dawn—to seal the promise that all
   93 will be well, to link Oberon's powers with the reality of daylight
       and to show their beneficence, to suggest that the events of the
       night are not a 'fruitless vision'?

396–9 *Up . . . down.* Is this a song of triumph, a charm, an incantation, a
       boasting?

400–2 *Here . . . thou.* Puck disguises his voice and moves rapidly from
       one part of the stage to another.

403–   *Lysander . . . way.* Lysander and Demetrius grope, stumble, and
   17 blunder in pursuit of each other.

Whiles I in this affair do thee employ,
I'll to my queen and beg her Indian boy:
And then I will her charmed eye release
From monster's view, and all things shall be peace.
PUCK: My fairy lord, this must be done with haste,
For night's swift dragons cut the clouds full fast,
And yonder shines Aurora's harbinger;   380
At whose approach, ghosts, wandering here and there,
Troop home to churchyards; damned spirits all,
That in crossways and floods have burial,
Already to their wormy beds are gone;
For fear lest day should look their shames upon,
They wilfully themselves exile from light,
And must for aye consort with black-browed night.
OBERON: But we are spirits of another sort.
I with the morning's love have oft made sport,
And like a forester the groves may tread,   390
Even till the eastern gate, all fiery-red,
Opening on Neptune with fair blessed beams,
Turns into yellow gold his salt green streams.
But, notwithstanding, haste, make no delay:
We may effect this business yet ere day.   *[Exit*
PUCK: Up and down, up and down,
I will lead them up and down:
I am feared in field and town.
Goblin, lead them up and down.
Here comes one.   400

Enter LYSANDER

LYSANDER: Where art thou, proud Demetrius? Speak thou now.
PUCK: Here villain, drawn and ready. Where art thou?
LYSANDER: I will be with thee straight.
PUCK: Follow me then
To plainer ground.   *[Exit Lysander following the voice*

409   *recreant*, coward.
410   *defiled*, disgraced.

418   *And . . . me*. Puck places the lovers appropriately on the stage.

420   *spite*, injury, wrong.

421   *Ho, ho, ho!* Puck's traditional laugh as he played pranks on humans.
422   *wot*, know.

426   *buy*, pay for.

Act Three, Scene Two

Enter DEMETRIUS

DEMETRIUS: Lysander, speak again.
 Thou runaway, thou coward, art thou fled?
 Speak! In some bush? Where dost thou hide thy head?
PUCK: Thou coward, art thou bragging to the stars,
 Telling the bushes that thou look'st for wars.
 And wilt not come? Come recreant, come thou child,
 I'll whip thee with a rod. He is defiled   410
 That draws a sword on thee.
DEMETRIUS: Yea, art thou there?
PUCK: Follow my voice; we'll try no manhood here.

                                        [*Exeunt*

Enter LYSANDER

LYSANDER: He goes before me and still dares me on.
 When I come where he calls, then he is gone.
 The villain is much lighter-heeled than I,
 I followed fast, but faster he did fly;
 That fallen am I in dark uneven way,
 And here will rest me. [*Lies down.*] Come thou gentle day,
 For if but once thou show me thy grey light,
 I'll find Demetrius and revenge this spite.   [*Sleeps*

Enter PUCK *and* DEMETRIUS

PUCK: Ho, ho, ho! Coward, why comest thou not?   421
DEMETRIUS: Abide me if thou darest, for well I wot
 Thou runn'st before me, shifting every place,
 And darest not stand, nor look me in the face.
 Where are thou now?
PUCK: Come hither; I am here.
DEMETRIUS: Nay then thou mock'st me. Thou shalt buy this
    dear,
 If ever I thy face by daylight see.

428–9 *Now . . . bed.* Is this due to weariness or to spells woven by Puck?
If the latter what actions are appropriate?

435 *sleep . . . eye.* The healing and consoling powers of sleep are
frequently mentioned by Shakespeare and his contemporaries.
436 *Steal . . . company,* i.e. as the others detest her company so she too
also wishes to be free from her own sorrowful company.
437–8 *Yet . . . four.* Is this a spell or an arithmetical statement?

439 *curst.* Perhaps 'under the curse or spell of love'.

448–
63 *On . . . well.* Puck's version of Oberon's instructions and blessing.

Now, go thy way. Faintness constraineth me
To measure out my length on this cold bed.
By day's approach look to be visited.   430

[Lies down and sleeps

Enter HELENA

HELENA: O weary night, O long and tedious night,
    Abate thy hours. Shine comforts from the east,
That I may back to Athens by daylight,
    From these that my poor company detest.
And sleep, that sometimes shuts up sorrow's eye,
Steal me awhile from mine own company.

[Lies down and sleeps

PUCK: Yet but three? Come one more.
          Two of both kinds makes up four.
          Here she comes, curst and sad.
          Cupid is a knavish lad,   440
          Thus to make poor females mad.

Enter HERMIA

HERMIA: Never so weary, never so in woe,
      Bedabbled with the dew, and torn with briers,
  I can no further crawl, no further go;
      My legs can keep no pace with my desires.
Here will I rest me till the break of day.
Heavens shield Lysander, if they mean a fray.

[Lies down and sleeps

PUCK: On the ground
          Sleep sound;
          I'll apply   450
          To your eye,
       Gentle lover, remedy.

[Puts the juice on Lysander's eyes
          When thou wak'st,

463   *The . . . well.* Another country proverb. *mare*, wife.

> Thou tak'st
> True delight
> In the sight
> Of thy former lady's eye.
> And the country proverb known,
> That every man should take his own,
> In your waking shall be shown.   460
> Jack shall have Jill;
> Nought shall go ill;
> The man shall have his mare again, and all shall be well.

[Exit

The wood

The placing of the players is important. The lovers are presumably back stage (l. 135), possibly in the discovery space or in an arbour. Is some property required for the 'flowery bed'?

Bottom is led in by Titania and the fairies.

2   *amiable*, lovable, lovely. *coy*, stroke.
3   *musk-roses*, scented wild roses.

5–7   *Where's . . . Peaseblossom.* Bottom's request is an anti-climax after Titania's loving attentions. Is Titania put out, too infatuated to notice? Does she continue to caress him?

10   *monsieur.* Bottom's attempt at courtesy as to a superior. See also 'signior' and 'Cavalery' ll. 16, 21.

13   *fret*, damage, injure.

18   *neaf*, fist.
19   *leave your courtesy.* Mustardseed is bowing hat in hand. Bottom acting as consort to the Fairy Queen enjoys giving orders and showing graciousness.
21   *Cavalery*, cavalero, cavalier.
21–2   *Cobweb*, ? Peaseblossom. See l. 7.
22–3   *I . . . face.* A possible allusion to Robert Greene who was amiable and hairy about the face.

ACT FOUR

SCENE ONE

LYSANDER, DEMETRIUS, HELENA, *and* HERMIA *lying asleep*

Enter TITANIA *and* BOTTOM; PEASEBLOSSOM, COBWEB, MOTH, MUSTARDSEED, *and other Fairies attending*; OBERON *behind unseen.*

TITANIA: Come sit thee down upon this flowery bed,
   While I thy amiable cheeks do coy,
   And stick musk-roses in thy sleek smooth head,
   And kiss thy fair large ears, my gentle joy.

BOTTOM: Where's Peaseblossom?

PEASEBLOSSOM: Ready.

BOTTOM: Scratch my head, Peaseblossom. Where's Monsieur Cobweb?

COBWEB: Ready.   9

BOTTOM: Monsieur Cobweb, good monsieur, get you your weapons in your hand, and kill me a red-hipped humble-bee on the top of a thistle; and good monsieur, bring me the honey-bag. Do not fret yourself too much in the action, monsieur; and good monsieur, have a care the honey-bag break not, I would be loth to have you overflown with a honey-bag signior. Where's Monsieur Mustardseed?

MUSTARDSEED: Ready.

BOTTOM: Give me your neaf, Monsieur Mustardseed. Pray you, leave your courtesy, good monsieur.

MUSTARDSEED: What's your will?   20

BOTTOM: Nothing good monsieur, but to help Cavalery Cobweb to scratch. I must to the barber's, monsieur, for methinks

25   *wilt . . . love*. Possibly Titania has in mind music that is the 'food of love'.

27   *tongs*, a musical instrument like a triangle. *bones*, pairs of flat bone strips held between the fingers and flicked together.
The Folio has the stage direction 'Music. Tongs. Rural music' which seems to be an addition for later performances.

28   *Or . . . eat*. Is this a hurried attempt to avoid the music of tongs and bones or is Titania just continuing to try to entertain him?

30   *bottle*, bundle.

31   *fellow*, equal.

33   *thee new*. Some editors read 'thee thence new' in order to keep the right length of line.

35   *exposition*, disposition.

39   *woodbine*, honeysuckle—in apposition to sweet honeysuckle.

40   *female ivy*, i.e. as clinging to the elm.

41   *barky fingers*. Possibly the deep corrugations of elm-bark.
The comedy of this scene arises from the absurdity of Titania's wooing of an ass, Bottom's unmusical ear and his desire for a donkey diet, his preference for scratching rather than caressing, and the anti-climaxes of his stolid unresponsiveness to the allurements of Titania.

46   *favours*, love-gifts.

I am marvellous hairy about the face. And I am such a tender
ass, if my hair do but tickle me, I must scratch.

TITANIA: What, wilt thou hear some music, my sweet love?

BOTTOM: I have a reasonable good ear in music. Let's have the
tongs and the bones.

TITANIA: Or say, sweet love, what thou desirest to eat.

BOTTOM: Truly a peck of provender. I could munch your good
dry oats. Methinks I have a great desire to a bottle of hay.
Good hay, sweet hay, hath no fellow.   31

TITANIA: I have a venturous fairy that shall seek
The squirrel's hoard, and fetch thee new nuts.

BOTTOM: I had rather have a handful or two of dried peas. But,
I pray you, let none of your people stir me. I have an exposition
of sleep come upon me.

TITANIA: Sleep thou, and I will wind thee in my arms.
Fairies be gone, and be all ways away.   [*Exeunt fairies*
So doth the woodbine, the sweet honeysuckle,
Gently entwist; the female ivy so   40
Enrings the barky fingers of the elm.
O how I love thee! How I dote on thee!   [*They sleep*

Enter PUCK

OBERON: [*Advancing*] Welcome, good Robin. See'st thou this
sweet sight?
Her dotage now I do begin to pity.
For meeting her of late behind the wood,
Seeking sweet favours for this hateful fool,
I did upbraid her and fall out with her.
For she his hairy temples then had rounded
With coronet of fresh and fragrant flowers.
And that same dew, which sometime on the buds   50
Was wont to swell like round and orient pearls,
Stood now within the pretty flowerets' eyes
Like tears that did their own disgrace bewail.

60   *hateful imperfection*. See II. i, 258, 'hateful fantasies'.

65   *accidents*, happenings.

70   *Dian's bud*, II. i, 183–4, i.e. Chaste tree. *Cupid's flower*, love-in-
      idleness. See II, i, 168.

73–4 *My . . . ass*. Does Titania awake in fear, alarm, surprise, laughter?
      What movements reveal her mood?

77   *Silence awhile*. Is this so that a charm can be made, to avoid arous-
      ing the lovers, to postpone the explanations to Titania's excited
      inquiry? *Robin . . . head*. Any magical performance?
s.d. *Music still*, i.e. still music. This direction occurs in the Folio. Pre-
      sumably it means that while Puck is busy with Bottom music
      sounds softly, and then ceases before Oberon calls for dance-
      music. What instruments are appropriate—viols, recorders or
      lutes?

When I had at my pleasure taunted her,
And she in mild terms begged my patience,
I then did ask of her her changeling child,
Which straight she gave me, and her fairy sent
To bear him to my bower in Fairyland.
And now I have the boy, I will undo
This hateful imperfection of her eyes.   60
And, gentle Puck, take this transformed scalp
From off the head of this Athenian swain;
That he, awaking when the other do,
May all to Athens back again repair,
And think no more of this night's accidents,
But as the fierce vexation of a dream.
But first I will release the Fairy Queen.
          Be as thou wast wont to be;
          See as thou wast wont to see.
          Dian's bud o'er Cupid's flower   70
          Hath such force and blessed power.
Now my Titania, wake you, my sweet queen.
TITANIA: My Oberon, what visions have I seen!
Methought I was enamoured of an ass.
OBERON: There lies your love.
TITANIA: How came these things to pass?
O, how mine eyes do loathe his visage now.
OBERON: Silence awhile. Robin, take off this head.
Titania, music call, and strike more dead
Than common sleep of all these five the sense.
TITANIA: Music, ho! music, such as charmeth sleep.   80
                                [Music still
PUCK: Now, when thou wak'st, with thine own fool's eyes
    peep.
OBERON: Sound, music. Come my queen, take hands with me,
And rock the ground whereon these sleepers be.
Now thou and I are new in amity,

85   *solemnly*, formally, with stately ceremony.

87   *prosperity*. The reading of the first Quarto. Some editors prefer 'posterity', the reading of the second Quarto and the Folio.

92   *silence sad*. Perhaps without music and song. See note to III. i, 179.

100– What is the dramatic value of these speeches—to signify by the
24   musical concord out of discord that all is now to be resolved in harmony, to establish Theseus and Hippolyta both in their classical setting and in the Elizabethan present, to drive away as it were darkness and evil, to appeal to the taste of the audience for hunting?

100   *forester*, huntsman.

101   *observation*, i.e. the observance to a morn of May (I. i, 167). Elizabeth herself went Maying at Highgate as late as 1601. See ll. 129–30.

102   *vaward*, forefront, early part.

109   *Hercules*. The celebrated hero of classical myth was associated according to some legends with Theseus in an expedition against the Amazons. *Cadmus*, the mythical founder of Thebes.

110   *bayed*, brought to bay, cornered, ran to earth.

111   *hounds of Sparta*. A celebrated breed according to Ovid and Virgil.

112   *gallant chiding*, fine baying.

114   *mutual*, related, linked, all-embracing.

And will tomorrow midnight solemnly
Dance in Duke Theseus' house triumphantly
And bless it to all fair prosperity.
There shall the pairs of faithful lovers be
Wedded, with Theseus, all in jollity.

PUCK: Fairy King, attend, and mark,   90
        I do hear the morning lark.
OBERON: Then, my queen, in silence sad,
        Trip we after night's shade.
        We the globe can compass soon,
        Swifter than the wandering moon.
TITANIA: Come my lord, and in our flight,
        Tell me how it came this night
        That I sleeping here was found
        With these mortals on the ground.   *[Exeunt*
                                              [Wind horns

      Enter THESEUS, HIPPOLYTA, EGEUS, *and train*

THESEUS: Go one of you, find out the forester;   100
For now our observation is performed,
And since we have the vaward of the day,
My love shall hear the music of my hounds.
Uncouple in the western valley, let them go.
Dispatch I say, and find the forester.   *[Exit an attendant*
We will, fair queen, up to the mountain's top,
And mark the musical confusion
Of hounds and echo in conjunction.
HIPPOLYTA: I was with Hercules and Cadmus once,
When in a wood of Crete they bayed the bear   110
With hounds of Sparta; never did I hear
Such gallant chiding. For, besides the groves,
The skies, the fountains, every region near
Seemed all one mutual cry. I never heard
So musical a discord, such sweet thunder.
THESEUS: My hounds are bred out of the Spartan kind,

117   *So . . . sanded*, with the same hanging chaps and the same sandy
       colour.
119   *dew-lapped*, with a hanging fold of skin at the throat.
120   *matched . . . bells*. Markham a contemporary of Shakespeare,
       recommended that in selecting hounds for a pack the pitch of their
       crying should be so matched that a pleasing harmony was heard
       when they were in full cry.
122   *hollaed*, 'holla', a huntsman's call to the hounds.

131   *in . . . solemnity*, to grace our observances.
132-3 *is . . . choice*. See Introduction, p. 5.

136-7 *Saint . . . now*. Traditionally birds mated on St Valentine's day, and
       the first person a young girl or man met would be their love. Is
       Theseus—ironic, sarcastic, amused, teasing, jesting?
138   *Pardon, my lord*. The lovers kneel.

So flewed, so sanded, and their heads are hung
With ears that sweep away the morning dew,
Crook-kneed, and dew-lapped like Thessalian bulls;
Slow in pursuit, but matched in mouth like bells,   120
Each under each. A cry more tuneable
Was never hollaed to, nor cheered with horn,
In Crete, in Sparta, nor in Thessaly.
Judge when you hear. But soft, what nymphs are these?
EGEUS: My lord, this is my daughter here asleep,
    And this, Lysander, this Demetrius is,
    This Helena, old Nedar's Helena.
    I wonder of their being here together.
THESEUS: No doubt they rose up early to observe
    The rite of May; and hearing our intent,   130
    Came here in grace of our solemnity.
    But speak, Egeus, is not this the day
    That Hermia should give answer of her choice?
EGEUS: It is, my lord.
THESEUS: Go bid the huntsmen wake them with their horns.
              [*Wind horns. Shout within. They all start up*
    Good morrow, friends. Saint Valentine is past.
    Begin these wood-birds but to couple now?
LYSANDER: Pardon, my lord.
THESEUS: I pray you all, stand up.
    I know you two are rival enemies.
    How comes this gentle concord in the world,   140
    That hatred is so far from jealousy,
    To sleep by hate, and fear no enmity?
LYSANDER: My lord, I shall reply amazedly,
    Half sleep, half waking. But as yet, I swear,
    I cannot truly say how I came here.
    But as I think—for truly would I speak,
    And now I do bethink me, so it is—
    I came with Hermia hither. Our intent

150   *Without . . . law*, be in no danger from.
151–6 *Enough . . . wife*. Do Egeus' repetitions suggest that he is—excitable, furious, garrulous?

164   *idle gaud*, empty pretence, useless toy.
165–   *Which . . . it*. With some dramatic irony Demetrius, unaware of
  73   the love juice on his eyes, explains that he is now, as it were,
       mature in judgement and restored to health.

Was to be gone from Athens, where we might
Without the peril of the Athenian law—   150
EGEUS: Enough, enough, my lord, you have enough:
   I beg the law, the law, upon his head.
   They would have stolen away, they would, Demetrius,
   Thereby to have defeated you and me,
   You of your wife, and me of my consent,
   Of my consent that she should be your wife.
DEMETRIUS: My lord, fair Helen told me of their stealth,
   Of this their purpose hither to this wood;
   And I in fury hither followed them,
   Fair Helena in fancy following me.   160
   But, my good lord, I wot not by what power
   But by some power it is—my love to Hermia,
   Melted as the snow, seems to me now
   As the remembrance of an idle gaud,
   Which in my childhood I did dote upon.
   And all the faith, the virtue of my heart,
   The object and the pleasure of mine eye,
   Is only Helena. To her, my lord,
   Was I betrothed ere I saw Hermia;
   But, like a sickness, did I loathe this food;   170
   But, as in health, come to my natural taste,
   Now I do wish it, love it, long for it,
   And will for evermore be true to it.
THESEUS: Fair lovers, you are fortunately met.
   Of this discourse we more will hear anon.
   Egeus, I will overbear your will;
   For in the temple, by and by, with us
   These couples shall eternally be knit.
   And, for the morning now is something worn,
   Our purposed hunting shall be set aside.   180
   Away with us to Athens, three and three,
   We'll hold a feast in great solemnity.

184– *These . . . dreams.* What is the dramatic purpose of this conversa-
96 tion when the lovers could have accompanied Theseus—to resolve
their relationships, to provide a light touch of comedy from their
bewilderment, to show their acceptance of their adventures as
dreams?

197–8 *When . . . Pyramus.* Bottom continues the rehearsal. All that
intervened from the moment Puck gave him the ass's head he
regards as a dream.

198– *Heigh-ho . . . asleep.* What gestures, movements and speech varia-
200 tion are appropriate as yawning gives way to surprise?

205 *patched fool*, a fool in parti-coloured dress. Perhaps the sense intended is utter fool.

206–8 *The . . . was.* Editors refer to *1 Corinthians*, ii. 9, which they allege
Bottom is parodying. Wilson adds that Bottom as a weaver
would be of a puritanical turn of mind. Other comment suggests
that this is Bottom's moment of glory, that like St. Paul he has
glimpsed hidden spiritual mysteries which defy the powers of the
senses to understand and refers to *2 Corinthians*, xii. 1–6, *1
Corinthians*, i. 27, *1 John*, i. 1. Reference might also be made to
Isaiah, lxiv. 4 where 'perceived by the ear' is suggestive.

209 *a . . . dream.* Unusual events, scandals, curiosities were frequently
recounted in ballad form and printed on broadsheets for sale.

210 *hath no bottom*, incapable of interpretation. In plays produced by
children like Edwards' *Damon & Pithias* the death of the hero or
heroine was inevitably accompanied by a death-song.

212 *her*, Thisby's.

Come Hippolyta.   *[Exeunt Theseus, Hippolyta,*
                                              Egeus, and train

DEMETRIUS: These things seem small and undistinguishable,
  Like far-off mountains turned into clouds.

HERMIA: Methinks I see these things with parted eye,
  When every thing seems double.

HELENA: So methinks.
  And I have found Demetrius like a jewel,
  Mine own, and not mine own.

DEMETRIUS: Are you sure
  That we are awake? It seems to me   190
  That yet we sleep, we dream. Do not you think
  The duke was here, and bid us follow him?

HERMIA: Yea, and my father.

HELENA: And Hippolyta.

LYSANDER: And he did bid us follow to the temple.

DEMETRIUS: Why then we are awake, let's follow him.
  And by the way let us recount our dreams.   *[Exeunt*

BOTTOM: [*Awaking*) When my cue comes, call me, and I will
answer. My next is, 'Most fair Pyramus'. Heigh-ho. Peter
Quince! Flute the bellows-mender! Snouth the tinker! Starveling! God's my life, stolen hence, and left me asleep. I have had
a most rare vision. I have had a dream, past the wit of man to
say what dream it was. Man is but an ass, if he go about to ex-
pound this dream. Methought I was—there is no man can tell
what. Methought I was, and methought I had—but man is but
a patched fool, if he will offer to say what methought I had.
The eye of man hath not heard, the ear of man hath not seen,
man's hand is not able to taste, his tongue to conceive, nor his
heart to report, what my dream was. I will get Peter Quince to
write a ballad of this dream; it shall be called Bottom's Dream,
because it hath no bottom; and I will sing it in the latter end of
our play, before the duke. Peradventure, to make it the more
gracious, I shall sing it at her death.   212 *[Exit*

Quince's house

Is Quince vexed, patient, sorrowful, anxious?

4   *transported*, (*a*) carried off, (*b*) transformed.

8   *discharge*, perform.
9   *wit*, skill.

11   *person*, appearance.
11–12 *paramour*, lover.

15–17 *Masters . . . men*. How do the others react to this?

17   *we . . . men*, i.e. our fortunes would have been made.
18–19 *sixpence a day*. Perhaps an allusion to the Children of the Chapel whose allowance was sixpence a day. Some see a reference to the payment by Elizabeth of £20 a year to the playwright Preston for playing in *Dido* in 1564.

    With what actions do the 'mechanicals' greet Bottom's triumphant entry?

24   *courageous*, splendid, encouraging (Chambers).

Act Four, Scene Two

SCENE TWO

Enter QUINCE, FLUTE, SNOUT, *and* STARVELING

QUINCE: Have you sent to Bottom's house? Is he come home yet?

STARVELING: He cannot be heard of. Out of doubt he is transported.

FLUTE: If he come not, then the play is marred. It goes not forward, doth it?

QUINCE: It is not possible. You have not a man in all Athens able to discharge Pyramus but he.

FLUTE: No, he hath simply the best wit of any handicraft man in Athens. 10

QUINCE: Yea, and the best person too; and he is a very paramour for a sweet voice.

FLUTE: You must say 'paragon'. A paramour is, God bless us, a thing of naught.

Enter SNUG

SNUG: Masters, the duke is coming from the temple, and there is two or three lords and ladies more married. If our sport had gone forward, we had all been made men.

FLUTE: O sweet bully Bottom. Thus hath he lost sixpence a day during his life; he could not have 'scaped sixpence a day. An the duke had not given him sixpence a day for playing Pyramus, I'll be hanged. He would have deserved it. Sixpence a day in Pyramus, or nothing. 22

Enter BOTTOM

BOTTOM: Where are these lads? Where are these hearts?

QUINCE: Bottom! O most courageous day! O most happy hour!

BOTTOM: Masters, I am to discourse wonders, but ask me not

26   *not true Athenian*. Quarto reading. Some editors prefer the Folio reading 'no true Athenian'. Perhaps a glance at the interest in tales of the Athenians in *Acts*, xvii. 21.

     Is Bottom confused, bashful, mysterious, exuberant, contradictory, anxious to impress, or to rouse curiosity?

31   *pumps*, shoes. *presently*, immediately.

33   *preferred*, put forward (i.e. included on Philostrate's list).

36   *breath*, (*a*) breath, (*b*) voice.
37   *sweet comedy*. An ironic anticipation.

     Is the mechanicals' departure slow, riotous, tumultuous, dignified?

what; for if I tell you, I am not true Athenian. I will tell you every thing, right as it fell out.

QUINCE: Let us hear, sweet Bottom. 28

BOTTOM: Not a word of me. All that I will tell you is, that the duke hath dined. Get your apparel together, good strings to your beards, new ribbons to your pumps, meet presently at the palace, every man look o'er his part. For the short and the long is, our play is preferred. In any case let Thisby have clean linen; and let not him that plays the lion pare his nails, for they shall hang out for the lion's claws. And most dear actors, eat no onions nor garlic, for we are to utter sweet breath; and I do not doubt but to hear them say, it is a sweet comedy. No more words. Away, go away! 38 [*Exeunt*

A full ceremonial entry with all the pageantry befitting a court celebrating a royal wedding. Theseus leads Hippolyta to the throne. Where will this be placed so that both Theseus and the audience see clearly the performance of *Pyramus and Thisby*?

2   *More . . . true.* Is Theseus amused, scornful, sceptical, thoughtful?
3   *antique fables.* A touch of irony in that Theseus is himself part of one. *antique,* (*a*) fantastic, (*b*) ancient. *toys,* foolish tales.
4   *seething,* ceaselessly working, in a ferment.
5   *shaping fantasies,* inventive imaginations. *apprehend,* are aware of, perceive.
6   *comprehends,* takes in, grasps.
7   *the poet.* See Appendix, p. 177.
8   *compact,* (*a*) composed of, charged with, (*b*) united, in agreement.
11   *Helen's.* Helen of Troy was held to be the most beautiful woman in the world. *brow of Egypt,* a gipsy's swarthy face.
12   *fine frenzy,* intense enthusiasm, noble excitement of inspiration.
13   *Doth . . . heaven,* i.e. takes in the whole range of things celestial and things earthly. Sidney's *Apology for Poetry* has a similar thought: '. . . The Poet . . . lifted up with the vigour of his own invention doth grow in effect another nature in making things either better than Nature bringeth forth, or, quite anew, forms such as never were in Nature . . . so as he goeth hand in hand with Nature, not enclosed within the narrow warrant of her gifts, but freely ranging onely within the Zodiac of his own wit.' The poet, who was held to be divinely inspired, may have been introduced to balance the demoniac inspiration of the lunatic.
14   *bodies forth,* creates, gives birth to.
16   *airy nothing,* idea, imagining, inspiration. Is Theseus contemptuous?

ACT FIVE

SCENE ONE

Enter THESEUS, HIPPOLYTA, PHILOSTRATE, LORDS, *and*
ATTENDANTS

HIPPOLYTA: 'T is strange, my Theseus, that these lovers speak of.
THESEUS: More strange than true. I never may believe
  These antique fables, nor these fairy toys.
  Lovers and madmen have such seething brains,
  Such shaping fantasies, that apprehend
  More than cool reason ever comprehends.
  The lunatic, the lover, and the poet
  Are of imagination all compact.
  One sees more devils than vast hell can hold,
  That is the madman. The lover, all as frantic,   10
  Sees Helen's beauty in a brow of Egypt.
  The poet's eye, in a fine frenzy rolling,
  Doth glance from heaven to earth, from earth to heaven;
  And as imagination bodies forth
  The forms of things unknown, the poet's pen
  Turns them to shapes, and gives to airy nothing
  A local habitation and a name.
  Such tricks hath strong imagination,

19–20 *if . . . joy*, if the mere idea of joy occurs to the imagination, it creates something or some person who causes that joy.

19 *apprehend*, entertain the idea.

20 *comprehends*, includes, conceives, brings about.

How does the description of the poet's creative power fit into Theseus' argument? Does he agree with Plato that poets are liars or is he praising them? Sidney wrote: 'The Poet never maketh any circles about your imagination to conjure you to believe for true what he writes.' Again he mentions a charge against Poets that 'they give names to men they write of, which argueth a conceit of an actual truth, and so, not being true, proves a falsehood'.

24 *transfigured so together*, changed. An apt image reminiscent of Bottom's dream.

25 *More . . . images*, is evidence of something more than the fantasies of imagination.

26 *grows . . . constancy*, unchanging, points to a consistent pattern of events.

27 *admirable*, wonderful.

28 *Here . . . mirth.* Any action by the lovers to justify this comment?

32 *masques.* The masque was a dramatic entertainment composed of music, poetry, and dancing, usually given in a private house. The players, who might be members of the household, wore masks.

34 *after-supper*, last course at supper. Supper began at about 5 p.m.

38 *Philostrate.* Philostrate is the Master of Revels at Theseus' court. The Master of Revels was an officer of Elizabeth's court who selected plays for performance before her. Actors' companies submitted their plays to him for censorship and a licence to perform. He supervised all productions at court.

39 *abridgement*, (*a*) short entertainment, (*b*) means of shortening the time.

42 *brief*, list.

44 *The . . . Centaurs.* Possibly the battle between the Lapithae and the Centaurs at the wedding of Pirithous, the close friend of Theseus who fought in the battle. Hercules was not present, though he did fight against the Centaurs. Immediately after the account of the battle in Ovid's *Metamorphoses* Nestor recounts some of Hercules' exploits in his honour. *Centaurs*, a mythical race of creatures, half horse, half man.

45 *eunuch*, castrato, a male singer with an unbroken voice.

That if it would but apprehend some joy,
It comprehends some bringer of that joy;   20
Or in the night, imagining some fear,
How easy is a bush supposed a bear!
HIPPOLYTA: But all the story of the night told over,
And all their minds transfigured so together,
More witnesseth than fancy's images,
And grows to something of great constancy;
But howsoever, strange and admirable.
THESEUS: Here come the lovers, full of joy and mirth.

Enter LYSANDER, DEMETRIUS, HERMIA, *and* HELENA
Joy, gentle friends, joy and fresh days of love
Accompany your hearts!
LYSANDER: More than to us   30
Wait in your royal walks, your board, your bed.
THESEUS: Come now; what masques, what dances shall we
have,
To wear away this long age of three hours
Between our after-supper and bed-time?
Where is our usual manager of mirth?
What revels are in hand? Is there no play,
To ease the anguish of a torturing hour?
Call Philostrate.
PHILOSTRATE: Here mighty Theseus.
THESEUS: Say, what abridgement have you for this evening?
What masque, what music? How shall we beguile   40
The lazy time, if not with some delight?
PHILOSTRATE: There is a brief how many sports are ripe.
Make choice of which your highness will see first.
                                           [*Gives a paper*
THESEUS: 'The battle with the Centaurs, to be sung
By an Athenian eunuch to the harp.'
We'll none of that. That have I told my love,

48–9   *tipsy . . . rage.* Orpheus, the famous minstrel of classical myth, mourning for the death of his bride, Eurydice, refused to play his lyre for some Thracian women who were celebrating the rites of Bacchus, the god of wine. In their frenzy they tore him to pieces and threw his head and lyre into the river Hebrus.

50   *device,* entertainment.

52–3   *The . . . beggary.* This may be no more than a jibe, common at the time, at the decay of learning through lack of patronage. However, commentators have suggested a reference to the death of Robert Greene (1592) who had attacked Shakespeare in his pamphlet *A Groatsworth of Wit,* 1592. Chambers thought that the death of Tasso (1595) was more likely to be intended. Others see a reference to Spenser's *Tears of the Muses,* 1592, followed by a parody of Spenser's style in Pyramus' final speech.

52   *thrice three Muses,* the nine goddesses who in classical myth were patrons of the arts.

56, 57   *tedious brief, tragical mirth.* Apart from the farcical contradiction this is perhaps a jest at the old fashioned morality plays, still popular perhaps with the unlettered, which had such advertisements as, *Appius and Virginia,* 'A new tragical comedy'; *Cambises,* A, lamentable Tragedy Mixed full of Pleasant Mirth'.

59   *wondrous strange snow.* Ironic.

61–70   *A . . . shed.* Is Philostrate—patronizing, smug, witty, scornful, amused, chuckling, sarcastic?

     Do the courtiers respond in any way to Philostrate's dramatic criticism?

74   *unbreathed,* untrained, unexercised.

79   *intents,* (*a*) endeavours, (*b*) subject matter.

In glory of my kinsman Hercules.
'The riot of the tipsy Bacchanals,
Tearing the Thracian singer in their rage.'
That is an old device, and it was played   50
When I from Thebes came last a conqueror.
'The thrice three Muses mourning for the death
Of learning, late deceased in beggary.'
That is some satire, keen and critical,
Not sorting with a nuptial ceremony.
'A tedious brief scene of young Pyramus
And his love Thisby; very tragical mirth.'
Merry and tragical? Tedious and brief?
That is, hot ice and wondrous strange snow.
How shall we find the concord of this discord?   60
PHILOSTRATE: A play there is, my lord, some ten words long,
Which is as brief as I have known a play;
But by ten words, my lord, it is too long,
Which makes it tedious. For in all the play
There is not one word apt, one player fitted.
And tragical, my noble lord, it is;
For Pyramus therein doth kill himself.
Which when I saw rehearsed, I must confess,
Made mine eyes water. But more merry tears
The passion of loud laughter never shed.   70
THESEUS: What are they that do play it?
PHILOSTRATE: Hard-handed men, that work in Athens here,
Which never laboured in their minds till now;
And now have toiled their unbreathed memories
With this same play, against your nuptial.
THESEUS: And we will hear it.
PHILOSTRATE: No my noble lord,
It is not for you. I have heard it over,
And it is nothing, nothing in the world;
Unless you can find sport in their intents,

80   *stretched*, strained. *conned*, learnt.

81–3   *I . . . it.* Is Theseus—generous, magnanimous, gracious, broad-minded, sympathetic?

85   *wretchedness o'ercharged*, poor people overwhelmed by undertaking too much.

86   *duty . . . perishing*, attempts to offer loyal service breaking down.
       Hippolyta out of sympathy for the mechanicals does not wish to see their failure exposed.

89   *The . . . nothing.* Theseus playfully quibbles on Hippolyta's 'nothing' and 'kind'.

90–2   *Our . . . merit*, we shall take our pleasure in their blunders, and what in their sense of duty they humbly try to do without success, we in nobility of mind will value it for the effort shown and not for its worth.

93–9   *Where . . . welcome.* Some see in these lines a compliment to Elizabeth and an allusion to her visits to Oxford or Cambridge where she was welcomed by lengthy addresses. Others suggest a reference to Elizabeth's visit to Warwick (1572) where she commended the Recorder for not being afraid of her, or her visit to Norwich (1578) where she encouraged the schoolmaster Limbert not to be afraid before he addressed her.

93   *clerks*, scholars, learned men.

96   *periods*, full stops.

97   *practised accent*, rehearsed delivery.

101   *fearful*, timid.

105   *In . . . capacity*, in the humblest pays me the greatest welcome according to the way I accept it.

106   *Prologue*, the actor who speaks the prologue. *addressed*, ready.

S.D.   *Flourish of trumpets.* The customary sign that a play was about to begin.

Extremely stretched and conned with cruel pain,   80
To do you service.

THESEUS: I will hear that play.
For never anything can be amiss,
When simpleness and duty tender it.
Go, bring them in, and take your places, ladies.

                          [Exit Philostrate

HIPPOLYTA: I love not to see wretchedness o'ercharged,
And duty in his service perishing.

THESEUS: Why gentle sweet, you shall see no such thing.

HIPPOLYTA: He says they can do nothing in this kind.

THESEUS: The kinder we, to give them thanks for nothing.
Our sport shall be to take what they mistake;   90
And what poor duty cannot do, noble respect
Takes it in might, not merit.
Where I have come, great clerks have purposed
To greet me with premeditated welcomes;
Where I have seen them shiver and look pale,
Make periods in the midst of sentences,
Throttle their practised accent in their fears,
And in conclusion dumbly have broke off,
Not paying me a welcome. Trust me sweet,
Out of this silence yet I picked a welcome;   100
And in the modesty of fearful duty
I read as much as from the rattling tongue
Of saucy and audacious eloquence.
Love, therefore, and tongue-tied simplicity
In least speak most, to my capacity.

             Enter PHILOSTRATE

PHILOSTRATE: So please your grace, the Prologue is addressed.

THESEUS: Let him approach.   *[Flourish of trumpets*

In a recent production Quince's scroll refused to remain unrolled, which supplied him with additional grounds for his mispunctuated reading.

111 *beginning . . . end*. Another felicitous pairing. See also ll. 162, 190–191, 216, 263.

118 *stand upon points*, (*a*) follow the punctuation, (*b*) trouble about fine distinctions.

119 *rid*, (*a*) ridden, (*b*) read, (*c*) thrown off. *rough*, unbroken.

120 *stop*, (*a*) punctuation mark, (*b*) sudden check by a horse. Horses were trained to stop suddenly by setting down both forelegs at the same time.

120–1 *it . . . true*. Lysander makes an epigram.

122–3 *like . . . recorder*, i.e. a child could not govern the stops (holes).

S.D. The Folio direction begins 'Tawyer with a trumpet before them . . .'. Tawyer (died 1625) was a 'hired man', servant to Heminges one of Shakespeare's fellow actors and compiler of the Folio edition. This direction probably refers to a later production of the play after the publication of the first Quarto.

How should the players enter—ceremonially, pompously, comically, disorderly, naively?

Quince presents his players who demonstrate what they have to do in mime. It is a kind of dumb show, but with the presenter explaining everything at length, there is nothing symbolic or 'inexplicable' about it.

127 *till . . . plain*, i.e. until the performance of the play explains the dumb show.

136 *did . . . scorn*, did . . . not despise.

Act Five, Scene One

Enter QUINCE *as* PROLOGUE

PROLOGUE: If we offend, it is with our good will.
    That you should think, we come not to offend,
    But with good will. To show our simple skill,   110
        That is the true beginning of our end.
    Consider then, we come but in despite.
        We do not come, as minding to content you,
    Our true intent is. All for your delight
        We are not here. That you should here repent you,
    The actors are at hand; and by their show,
    You shall know all, that you are like to know.
THESEUS: This fellow doth not stand upon points.
LYSANDER: He hath rid his prologue like a rough colt; he knows
    not the stop. A good moral, my lord: it is not enough to
    speak, but to speak true.   121
HIPPOLYTA: Indeed he hath played on his prologue like a child
    on a recorder, a sound, but not in government.
THESEUS: His speech was like a tangled chain; nothing im-
    paired, but all disordered. Who is next?

Enter PYRAMUS *and* THISBY, WALL, MOONSHINE,
and LION

PROLOGUE: Gentles, perchance you wonder at this show,
    But wonder on, till truth make all things plain.
    This man is Pyramus, if you would know;
        This beauteous lady Thisby is certain.
    This man, with lime and rough-cast, doth present   130
        Wall, that vile Wall which did these lovers sunder;
    And through Wall's chink, poor souls, they are content
        To whisper. At the which let no man wonder.
    This man, with lanthorn, dog, and bush of thorn,
        Presenteth Moonshine. For if you will know,
    By moonshine did these lovers think no scorn
        To meet at Ninus' tomb, there, there to woo.

153

138   *hight*, is called.

143   *tall*, fine.

145–6 *Whereat ... breast*. This excessive alliteration and the strained
        epithets are a glance at a style of writing that was popular in
        romantic poems.
146   *broached*, pierced (like a barrel).

154–   *In ... whisper*. Is this to be read from a scroll as a prologue?
  63

162   *sinister*, (*a*) left, (*b*) threatening. See note to l. 111.
163   *whisper*. An anticlimax of a rhyme.
164   *Would ... better*. Theseus speaks well of Wall, i.e. it is not to be
        expected that a wall would make a better speech. *lime and hair*, the
        constituents of plaster.
165   *partition*, (*a*) wall, (*b*) division into parts of a subject under discus-
        sion.
            Does Pyramus enter stealthily, with posturing, quickly,
        martially, cumbered with equipment?
168–   *O ... me*. A burlesque of some popular verse writing with its
  79   frequent apostrophes. See *Phoenix Nest*, 1593, 'O night, o jealous
        night, etc.'.

This grisly beast, which Lion hight by name,
The trusty Thisby, coming first by night,
Did scare away, or rather did affright.   140
And as she fled, her mantle she did fall,
    Which Lion vile with bloody mouth did stain.
Anon comes Pyramus, sweet youth, and tall,
    And finds his trusty Thisby's mantle slain.
Whereat, with blade, with bloody blameful blade,
    He bravely broached his boiling bloody breast.
And Thisby, tarrying in mulberry shade,
    His dagger drew, and died. For all the rest,
Let Lion, Moonshine, Wall, and lovers twain
At large discourse, while here they do remain.   150
  [*Exeunt Prologue, Pyramus, Thisby, Lion, and Moonshine*
THESEUS: I wonder if the lion be to speak.
DEMETRIUS: No wonder, my lord. One lion may, when many
asses do.
WALL: In this same interlude it doth befall
    That I, one Snout by name, present a wall;
    And such a wall, as I would have you think,
    That had in it a crannied hole or chink,
    Through which the lovers, Pyramus and Thisby,
    Did whisper often very secretly.
    This loam, this rough-cast, and this stone doth show   160
    That I am that same wall; the truth is so.
    And this the cranny is, right and sinister,
    Through which the fearful lovers are to whisper.
THESEUS: Would you desire lime and hair to speak better?
DEMETRIUS: It is the wittiest partition, that ever I heard dis-
course, my lord.

Enter PYRAMUS

THESEUS: Pyramus draws near the wall: silence!
PYRAMUS: O grim-looked night! O night with hue so black!

174-5 *O wall . . . eyne*. Any response from Wall to this praise?

180 *sensible*, having senses or understanding.

182-5 *No . . . comes*. Is this—friendliness, anxiety, failure to understand play-acting, naivety, bumptiousness, irrelevance?

190-1 *I . . . face*. For a similar confusion of the senses see IV. i, 206-8; III. i, 79.

194 *grace*. A title of high rank.

195 *Limander*, i.e. Leander who according to classical story was drowned while swimming the Hellespont to visit his love Hero.

196 *Helen*. Perhaps Quince's knowledge is faulty and he confuses Hero with Helen of Troy—not the most trusty of ladies! *Fates*. In classical myth they were three in number, Clotho, Lachesis and Atropos, who wove the threads of man's life and finally cut off the finished pattern.

197 *Shafalus to Procrus*. Ovid in his *Metamorphoses* told how an Athenian Cephalus married to Procis was wooed in vain by Aurora goddess of the dawn.

O night, which ever art when day is not!
O night, O night, alack, alack, alack,   170
   I fear my Thisby's promise is forgot!
And thou, O wall, O sweet, O lovely wall,
   That stand'st between her father's ground and mine!
Thou wall, O wall, O sweet and lovely wall,
   Show me thy chink, to blink through with mine eyne!
                          [Wall holds up his fingers
Thanks, courteous wall. Jove shield thee well for this.
   But what see I? No Thisby do I see.
O wicked wall, through whom I see no bliss,
   Cursed be thy stones for thus deceiving me!
THESEUS: The wall methinks, being sensible, should curse
   again.   181
PYRAMUS: No in truth, sir, he should not. 'Deceiving me' is
   Thisby's cue. She is to enter now, and I am to spy her through
   the wall. You shall see, it will fall pat as I told you. Yonder
   she comes.

Enter THISBY

THISBY: O wall, full often hast thou heard my moans,
   For parting my fair Pyramus and me!
My cherry lips have often kissed thy stones,
   Thy stones with lime and hair knit up in thee.
PYRAMUS: I see a voice; now will I to the chink,   190
   To spy an I can hear my Thisby's face.
   Thisby!
THISBY: My love thou art, my love I think.
PYRAMUS: Think what thou wilt, I am thy lover's grace,
   And, like Limander, am I trusty still.
THISBY: And I like Helen, till the Fates me kill.
PYRAMUS: Not Shafalus to Procrus was so true.
THISBY: As Shafalus to Procrus, I to you.
PYRAMUS: O kiss me through the hole of this vile wall.

202   '*Tide*, come.

205   *mural down*. A much debated reading. The Folio has 'morall downe', the Quarto 'Moon used'. Sisson suggests 'moon to see'.

206–7   *when . . . warning*. An allusion to the proverb 'walls have ears'.

209   *shadows*, actors, representations.

214   *moon*. Quartos and Folios have 'man'. Wilson's note is apposite 'Theseus has just remarked that Quince's company of actors 'may pass for excellent men', and the jest in the sudden transition from this to 'here come two noble *beasts* in' would be blunted altogether if we read 'a man and a lion'.

215–22   *You . . . life*. Is this a prologue read from a scroll?

216   *smallest monstrous*. See note to l. 111.

219   *as*, Quarto reading, 'one', Folio.

220   *fell*, fierce, i.e. it is only as Snug the joiner playing his part that I am a terrible lion, and not otherwise. Some editors take 'fell' as 'skin'. *lion's dam*. A remarkable possibility—out of consideration for the ladies?

224   *best . . . beast*. A frequent pun.
        fox. Regarded as cowardly.

227–30   *for . . . fox*. A play on the proverb 'the better part of valour is discretion'.

THISBY: I kiss the wall's hole, not your lips at all.   200
PYRAMUS: Wilt thou at Ninny's tomb meet me straightway?
THISBY: 'Tide life, 'tide death, I come without delay.
                              [*Exeunt Pyramus and Thisby*
WALL: Thus have I, Wall, my part discharged so;
   And, being done, thus Wall away doth go.   [*Exit*
THESEUS: Now is the mural down between the two neighbours.
DEMETRIUS: No remedy my lord, when walls are so wilful to
   hear without warning.
HIPPOLYTA: This is the silliest stuff that ever I heard.
THESEUS: The best in this kind are but shadows; and the worst
   are no worse, if imagination amend them.   210
HIPPOLYTA: It must be your imagination then, and not theirs.
THESEUS: If we imagine no worse of them than they of them-
   selves, they may pass for excellent men. Here come two noble
   beasts in, a moon and a lion.

Enter LION *and* MOONSHINE

LION: You ladies, you, whose gentle hearts do fear
   The smallest monstrous mouse that creeps on floor,
May now perchance both quake and tremble here,
   When lion rough in wildest rage doth roar.
Then know that I, as Snug the joiner am
A lion fell, nor else no lion's dam;   220
For if I should as lion come in strife
Into this place, 't were pity on my life.
THESEUS: A very gentle beast, and of a good conscience.
DEMETRIUS: The very best at a beast, my lord, that e'er I saw.
LYSANDER: This lion is a very fox for his valour.
THESEUS: True; and a goose for his discretion.
DEMETRIUS: Not so my lord, for his valour cannot carry his
   discretion, and the fox carries the goose.
THESEUS: His discretion, I am sure, cannot carry his valour;
   for the goose carries not the fox. It is well. Leave it to his

232-7   *This . . . be.* Is this a prologue read from a scroll?
232   *lanthorn . . . horned.* Hence the aptness of 'lan*thorn*'!
233   *He . . . head,* i.e. as a cuckold, a man whose wife is unfaithful.

237   *seem to be,* represent, have the appearance of. See III. i, 16.

242   *in snuff,* (*a*) angry, (*b*) requiring trimming.

245   *small . . . discretion,* i.e. Moon is showing signs of annoyance.

249-   *All . . . dog.* In his anger he omits the verse.
51

258-9   *Well . . . grace.* Is Hippolyta ironic, sarcastic, mocking, gracious, forgetting her boredom (l. 243).

discretion, and let us listen to the moon.   231

MOONSHINE: This lanthorn doth the horned moon present—

DEMETRIUS: He should have worn the horns on his head.

THESEUS: He is no crescent, and his horns are invisible within
the circumference.

MOONSHINE: This lanthorn doth the horned moon present,
Myself the man i' th' moon do seem to be.

THESEUS: This is the greatest error of all the rest; the man should
be put into the lanthorn. How is it else the man i' th'
moon?   240

DEMETRIUS: He dares not come there for the candle. For you
see, it is already in snuff.

HIPPOLYTA: I am aweary of this moon. Would he would
change.

THESEUS: It appears by his small light of discretion, that he is in
the wane. But yet, in courtesy, in all reason, we must stay the
time.

LYSANDER: Proceed Moon.

MOONSHINE: All that I have to say, is to tell you that the
lanthorn is the moon, I the man in the moon, this thorn-bush,
my thorn-bush, and this dog my dog.   251

DEMETRIUS: Why all these should be in the lanthorn; for all
these are in the moon. But silence, here comes Thisby.

Enter THISBY

THISBY: This is old Ninny's tomb. Where is my love?

LION: [*Roars*] Oh—   [*Thisby runs off*

DEMETRIUS: Well roared, Lion.

THESEUS: Well run, Thisby.

HIPPOLYTA: Well shone, Moon. Truly the moon shines with a
good grace.   [*The Lion shakes Thisby's mantle, and exit*

THESEUS: Well moused, Lion.   260

DEMETRIUS: And then came Pyramus.

LYSANDER: And so the lion vanished.

263–   *Sweet . . . quell.* Again Shakespeare is parodying contemporary
  78   verse: 'Thy beams, the spiteful beams, Thy envious glaring
      gleams' (*Phoenix Nest*).

263   *sunny beams.* See note to l. 111.

265   *beams.* The Quarto reading. Some editors read 'gleams'. Sisson
      suggest a pause after 'glittering' and then the anticlimax of 'beams'
      —Bottom fails to remember the alliterating 'gleams'.

269   *dole,* grief.

272   *duck,* darling.

275   *Furies.* In classical myth three female spirits sent from the under-
      world to punish crime or avenge wrong-doing.

277   *thrum,* the unwoven end of a warp-thread cut off to remove the
      woven material from the loom.

278   *Quail,* destroy. *quell.* kill.

283   *deflowered,* violated. Bottom's error for 'devoured'.

286   *counfound,* be shed, pour out.

286–   *Come . . . die.* This lament and Thisby's later one may have been
  97   sung to the lute as, it appears, was the fashion.

289–   *pap, hop.* Which rhyme?
  90

Act Five, Scene One

Enter PYRAMUS

PYRAMUS: Sweet moon, I thank thee for they sunny beams.
   I thank thee, moon, for shining now so bright.
For by thy gracious, golden, glittering gleams,
   I trust to take of truest Thisby sight.
         But stay, O spite!
         But mark, poor knight,
      What dreadful dole is here!
         Eyes do you see?   270
         How can it be?
      O dainty duck! O dear!
         Thy mantle good,
         What, stained with blood!
      Approach ye Furies fell.
         O Fates, come, come,
         Cut thread and thrum,
      Quail, crush, conclude, and quell.
THESEUS: This passion, and the death of a dear friend, would go
  near to make a man look sad.   280
HIPPOLYTA: Beshrew my heart, but I pity the man.
PYRAMUS: O wherefore Nature, didst thou lions frame?
   Since lion vile hath here deflowered my dear.
  Which is—no, no—which was the fairest dame
   That lived, that loved, that liked, that looked with cheer.
         Come tears, confound.
         Out sword, and wound
        The pap of Pyramus;
         Ay, that left pap,
         Where heart doth hop.   *[Stabs himself*
        Thus die I, thus, thus, thus.   291
         Now am I dead,
         Now am I fled,
        My soul is in the sky.

297   *Now . . . die.* Arkwright (*Proc. Royal Mus. Assoc.*, 1913–14, pp. 117–36) notes similar endings in songs by Farrant and Edwards for plays performed by Children's Companies.

298   *die,* (*a*) dying, (*b*) dice. *ace,* (*a*) the one pip on a dice, (*b*) ass, (*c*) bad luck.

301   *ass.* A glance at 'ace' and at Bottom's metamorphosis.

305   *passion,* grief.

S.D.   Does she enter—trippingly, as a dainty duck, fearfully, in trouble with her garments?

308   *mote,* speck.

309–   *he . . . us,* i.e. may we be pardoned for mentioning Pyramus and
10   Thisby as presenting anything like a man and a woman.

312   *means,* (*a*) laments, (*b*) lodges an official legal complaint; 'videlicet' underlines the second sense. *videlicet,* namely. Used in legal and formal documents.

319–   *lily . . . leeks.* A parody of love poems of the period, and a nice
24   derangement of epithets.

325–   *O . . . silk.* Further parody, this time possibly of a passage in A
30   Sonnet in *A Handful of Pleasant Delights,* 1566.

> O Gods above, my faithful love,
>   Shall never fail this need,
> For this my breath by fatal death
>   Shall weave Atropos' thread.
> Then from his sheath he drew his blade
>   And to his heart
> He thrust the point, and life did vade
>   With painful smart.

Tongue lose thy light,
Moon take thy flight,   [*Exit Moonshine*
Now die, die, die, die, die.   [*Dies*

DEMETRIUS: No die, but an ace for him; for he is but one.

LYSANDER: Less than an ace, man; for he is dead, he is nothing.

THESEUS: With the help of a surgeon he might yet recover, and
prove an ass.   301

HIPPOLYTA: How chance Moonshine is gone before Thisby
comes back and finds her lover?

THESEUS: She will find him by starlight. Here she comes, and
her passion ends the play.

Enter THISBY

HIPPOLYTA: Methinks she should not use a long one for such a
Pyramus. I hope she will be brief.

DEMETRIUS: A mote will turn the balance, which Pyramus,
which Thisby, is the better: he for a man, God warrant us; she
for a woman, God bless us.

LYSANDER: She hath spied him already with those sweet eyes.

DEMETRIUS: And thus she means, videlicet—   312

THISBY: Asleep my love?
      What, dead, my dove?
   O Pyramus, arise.
      Speak, speak. Quite dumb?
      Dead, dead? A tomb
   Must cover thy sweet eyes.
      These lily lips,
      This cherry nose,   320
   These yellow cowslip cheeks,
      Are gone, are gone.
      Lovers, make moan.
   His eyes were green as leeks.
      O Sisters Three,
      Come, come to me,

333   *Come . . . imbrue*. Sharpham's play *The Fleir*, 1607 preserves a piece of contemporary stage business in the remark by one character: 'Faith, like Thisby in the play, a' has almost kill'd himself with the scabbard.' *imbrue*, stain with blood.

337–8   *Moonshine . . . too*. Dover Wilson suggests that originally Lion, Moonshine, and Wall entered here, as the Quarto's assignment of Bottom's speech to Lion suggests, for the purpose of drawing a curtain across the discovery space to hide the bodies, and to offer the Bergomask dance and the Epilogue.

339–   *No . . . company*. Folio gives this to Bottom, Quarto to Lion. The
41   revival of Pyramus and his rousing Thisby from his chest to contradict Theseus appears to be a highly effective bit of stage business added as an afterthought. It is quite in keeping with Bottom's nature and effectively disposes of the 'dead bodies'.

339–   *the . . . fathers*, i.e. their fathers are reconciled. Mr B. M. Forrest
40   drew my attention to a similar breaking down of a wall as a symbol of reconciliation in Terence's *Adelphi*, ll. 908–9. See *Ephesians*, ii. 14.

340–   *see . . . dance*. Bottom is still troubled by the senses. However, the
41   Bergamask may have been a song and dance.

340   *epilogue*. Should Bottom produce another scroll?

341   *Bergamask*, a clumsy country dance. Named after Bergamo, a country district in Italy.

347   *discharged*, performed.

S.D.   *A dance*. The Bergamask dance rounds off the comedy and acts as a foil to the fairy dancing to follow. It was probably accompanied by pipe and tabor.

349   *told*, (*a*) announced, (*b*) tolled.

350   *fairy time*. Earlier Theseus rejected 'fairy toys'. Perhaps this is said jestingly to tease the lovers.

With hands as pale as milk;
  Lay them in gore,
  Since you have shore
With shears his thread of silk.   330
  Tongue, not a word.
  Come, trusty sword;
Come blade, my breast imbrue.   [*Stabs herself*
  And farewell, friends,
  Thus Thisby ends:
Adieu, adieu, adieu.   [*Dies*

THESEUS: Moonshine and Lion are left to bury the dead.

DEMETRIUS: Ay, and Wall too.

BOTTOM: [*Starting up*] No, I assure you, the wall is down that parted their fathers. Will it please you to see the epilogue, or to hear a Bergamask dance between two of our company?   341

THESEUS: No epilogue, I pray you; for your play needs no excuse. Never excuse; for when the players are all dead, there need none to be blamed. Marry, if he that writ it had played Pyramus, and hanged himself in Thisby's garter, it would have been a fine tragedy. And so it is, truly, and very notably discharged. But come, your Bergamask. Let your epilogue alone.   [*A dance*

The iron tongue of midnight hath told twelve.
Lovers to bed, 'tis almost fairy time.   350

352   *overwatched*, stayed up late.

353–4 *This . . . night*, obviously this clumsy play has most suitably wiled away the laborious passage of night.

S.D.   A fully ceremonial departure emptying the stage.

357– *Now . . . glide*. Puck reminds the audience of the less pleasant but
68   more customary aspects of night. Why?

360   *fordone*, exhausted.

361   *brands*, logs.

370   *triple Hecate's team*, the threefold goddess Cynthia or Phoebe in the heavens, Diana or Artemis on earth, Hecate or Proserpine in the underworld. Hecate was sometimes regarded as Night. See *Henry V*, IV. i, 267, and *Lucrece*, l. 764. *team*, dragons.

374   *hallowed house*, i.e. the private house in which the play was being presented.

375–6 *I . . . door*. Puck like the presenter in some Mummers' plays sweeps out the dust from behind the door and cleanses the house of evil powers.

S.D.   Oberon, Titania, and the fairies enter to bless the house and the married couples. They carry lighted tapers. (See illustration, p. 19.)

I fear we shall out-sleep the coming morn,
As much as we this night have overwatched.
This palpable-gross play hath well beguiled
The heavy gait of night. Sweet friends, to bed.
A fortnight hold we this solemnity,
In nightly revels, and new jollity.   [*Exeunt*

Enter PUCK

PUCK: Now the hungry lion roars,
     And the wolf behowls the moon;
    Whilst the heavy ploughman snores,
     All with weary task fordone.   360
    Now the wasted brands do glow,
     Whilst the screech-owl, screeching loud,
    Puts the wretch that lies in woe
     In remembrance of a shroud.
    Now it is the time of night,
     That the graves all gaping wide,
    Every one lets forth his sprite,
     In the church-way paths to glide.
    And we fairies, that do run
     By the triple Hecate's team,   370
    From the presence of the sun,
     Following darkness like a dream,
    Now are frolic: not a mouse
    Shall disturb this hallowed house.
    I am sent with broom before,
    To sweep the dust behind the door.

Enter OBERON *and* TITANIA *with their train*

OBERON: Through the house give glimmering light,
    By the dread and drowsy fire,
    Every elf and fairy sprite
    Hop as light as bird from briar,   380

383   *by rote*, by heart, accurately.

387–   *Now . . . day*. There is disagreement over the song and dance.
408   Some editors follow the Folio which prints 'Now until, etc., in
      italics as the song, others follow the Quarto which assigns this as a
      speech to Oberon. Wilson, adding to Richmond Noble's argu-
      ment, indicates that Oberon sings 'Now . . . stray', the fairies join
      in 'To . . . be' (388–400). Oberon continues 'With . . . day'
      (401–8). In this way the instructions in ll. 381–2) ('after me'), 383
      (your = Oberon), 386 (we = Titania and fairies).

398   *prodigious*, of ill-omen.

401   *field-dew consecrate*. A fairy parallel to a former custom in which
      priests sometimes blessed the bridal bed and sprinkled it with holy
      water.

409   *shadows*, (*a*) actors, (*b*) spirits.

And this ditty after me,
Sing, and dance it trippingly.
TITANIA: First rehearse your song by rote,
To each word a warbling note.
Hand in hand, with fairy grace,
Will we sing, and bless this place.   [*Song and dance*
OBERON: Now, until the break of day,
Through this house each fairy stray.
To the best bride-bed will we,
Which by us shall blessed be.   390
And the issue there create,
Ever shall be fortunate.
So shall all the couples three
Ever true in loving be;
And the blots of Nature's hand
Shall not in their issue stand.
Never mole, hare lip, nor scar,
Nor mark prodigious, such as are
Despised in nativity,
Shall upon their children be.   400
With this field-dew consecrate,
Every fairy take his gait,
And each several chamber bless,
Through this palace, with sweet peace;
And the owner of it blest,
Ever shall in safety rest.
Trip away; make no stay;
Meet me all by break of day.
               [*Exeunt Oberon, Titania, and train*

EPILOGUE
PUCK: If we shadows have offended,
Think but this, and all is mended,   410
That you have but slumbered here,

171

414   *No . . . but,* offering you no more than.

419   *serpent's tongue,* hissing off the stage.

423   *hands,* (*a*) applause, (*b*) handshakes.

While these visions did appear.
And this weak and idle theme,
No more yielding but a dream,
Gentles, do not reprehend.
If you pardon, we will mend.
And, as I am an honest Puck,
If we have unearned luck
Now to 'scape the serpent's tongue,
We will make amends ere long;   420
Else the Puck a liar call.
So, good night unto you all.
Give me your hands, if we be friends,
And Robin shall restore amends.   *[Exit*

APPENDICES

I

THE SOURCES OF THE PLAY

A Midsummer Night's Dream has no single source; a diversity of strains has gone to its making.

Chaucer's *Knight's Tale* suggested the wedding of Theseus and Hippolyta, and from the same source came matter that prompted reference to May Day observances, the hunting scene, and some hint of the wisdom and magnanimity of Theseus' character. Perhaps the strife between Palamon and Arcite for Emily may have suggested the rivalry between Lysander and Demetrius, but the adventures of the lovers is probably a happy version of the Pyramus and Thisby story. North's translation of Plutarch's *Lives* provided the list of Theseus' former loves. The view that Pluto and Proserpine in Chaucer's *Merchant's Tale* provided matter for Oberon and Titania is not convincing.

The name Oberon comes from the medieval romance *Huon of Bordeaux*. He appears in Greene's play *James IV* (*c.* 1594) as spectator, chorus, and magician. He had previously appeared as Auberon with his queen Aureola in the entertainment given to Queen Elizabeth at Elvetham in 1591. Titania was a name used by Ovid for Diana whom the Middle Ages changed from a classical goddess to the queen of the fairies. Dover Wilson, postulating an early version of the play not by Shakespeare, draws a number of parallels between Oberon, Titania, and Puck and Venus, Psyche, and Cupid in Apuleius' *Golden Ass* translated by Adlington in 1566. Bottom's metamorphosis, too, may derive from the same work. In it Lucius, changed into an ass by enchantment, is passionately embraced by a woman of noble birth, and he is promised adornments and food by the imprisoned maiden Charite. The beautiful goddess Isis appears to him in a vision and promises him release from his ass's shape.

Some writers consider that Oberon's vision, II. i, 155–68, is a direct reference to the entertainment of Elizabeth at Kenilworth in 1575. The allusion to the 'fair vestal throned by the west' is certainly a tribute to her, but there are also resemblances to the Elvetham entertainment of

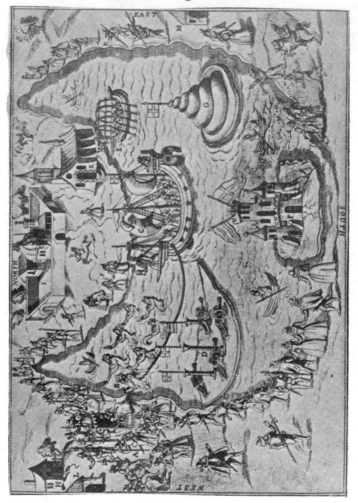

A WOODCUT OF THE ENTERTAINMENT GIVEN
TO QUEEN ELIZABETH I AT ELVETHAM, 1591

1592, and this, nearer in time to the play, with its dance of fairies, its fairy songs in 'eight and eight', and other similarities noted by Venezky has the stronger claim (see p. 176 for a contemporary illustration of the entertainment).

The rehearsal of the play within the play for presentation at wedding celebrations has a similarity in general terms to Munday's play *John a Kent and John a Cumber*, but there are no verbal links. The story of Pyramus and Thisby has many possible sources. It first appears in Ovid's *Metamorphoses*, Chaucer tells it in the *Legend of Good Women*, Lydgate and Gower recount it to illustrate the disaster that attends ungovernable physical love. English writers in the sixteenth century produced ballad versions in the anthologies *A Handful of Pleasant Delights*, 1584, and the *Gorgeous Gallery of Gallant Inventions*, 1562, and one by Gale appeared separately about 1596. Yet another version appeared in Thomas Mouffet's *Silkworms and their Flies*, 1599, which it is claimed was possibly available earlier in manuscript. Shakespeare knew Ovid's story in Latin and Golding's translation. It seems that he also remembered and used occasional words or phrases from the *Legend of Good Women* and the two versions in the anthologies. Muir claims that Shakespeare took most from Mouffet's poem, and he quotes a large number of parallels (*Shakespeare's Sources*, pp. 39–45). Other mythological ballads narrating other stories from Ovid have been cited by Bush as contributing to Shakespeare's version. Virtually all these late versions contain the same kind of ludicrous bad poetry that appears in the play. Muir suggests that Shakespeare was not only pillorying Mouffet, but that he has 'compiled a kind of anthology of bad poetry'. He also offers another inference: 'It is possible, of course, that all the versions of the Pyramus and Thisbe story Shakespeare had read since childhood coalesced in his mind; but the evidence suggests that he consulted them during the actual composition of *A Midsummer Night's Dream*.'

II

REVISIONS OF THE TEXT

IN the New Cambridge edition of the play (1924) Dover Wilson suggested that it contained three layers of writing of different date. The original play he would date 1592 or earlier, then followed a revision in 1596, and another for the wedding of Southampton to Elizabeth Vernon in 1598. He has recently repeated his views in *Shakespeare's Happy Comedies*, 1962, pp. 184–220, adding that the earliest version of the play may not have been written by Shakespeare, and that the play may have been performed at three other weddings.

The evidence to support these views is drawn mainly from allusions in the play to events that can be dated, textual inconsistencies and abnormalities, and marked variations in the style and quality of the verse. It should be said at once that the play written for private performance was given, for public performance later, an epilogue spoken by Puck (V. i, 409–24) to take the place of the fairy masque (V. i, 357–408) which previously concluded it. There are also signs of changes to the interlude: the casting of Starveling, Snout, and Quince in I. ii, 51–4 as parents of Pyramus and Thisby is silently dropped later on. Dover Wilson, however, maintains that the alternations between the speech-headings Puck and Robin in the Quarto edition show that those passages concerned with the love juice are associated with Puck, and not with Robin, and he assigns these passages to a revision. There are a number of instances in the text as well as in speech headings where this association does not hold, and the inference is therefore unconvincing. In V. i, 1–84 Wilson maintains that mislineations in the Quarto edition indicate that the compositor was incorporating additional matter written in the margin of his copy. He reinforces his argument by noting that the disturbed lines can be omitted without damaging the sense of the passage. Some doubts have been thrown on this last assertion by Kirschbaum. In a substantial article on the Quarto text by R. K. Turner, Jnr., in *Studies in Bibliography*, XV (1962) support is given to Wilson's view.

It is possible that the printer was in fact packing in six lines above his quota for the three quarto pages containing the mislineations, for the total effect is to include six lines of verse more than he would have done normally on these pages. When it is seen that the first of these pages together with the three that precede it contain the equivalent of six lines less than they should normally have done, it may well be that the mis-lineations are the compositor's device for covering bad casting off, and for rectifying an error in setting up the pages of the G gathering of the quarto in which all the short pages and mislinings occur. This assumes that the copy for the quarto was cast off by gatherings, and this seems to be the case. It also assumes that the compositor set up his pages seriatim, a less usual practice.

While there is evidence of alteration to the text, evidence for the wholesale revisions suggested by Dover Wilson is capable of simpler explanations that would avoid disintegrating the play and would preserve its essential unity.

III

SHAKESPEARE'S THEATRE

ALTHOUGH the evidence for the design of Elizabethan theatres is in-complete and conflicting, and although there were certainly differences of construction and arrangement, the following account, it is hoped, will give a reasonable outline.

The first public theatres in London were built during Shakespeare's lifetime. According to some they embodied in their design and construc-tion the experience and practice of the medieval and Tudor play pro-ductions in inn yards, booth stages, and pageant wagons. Recently Glynne Wickham has argued strongly against this view, claiming that the game-houses, tournament arenas, banqueting chamber and town-hall provide the basis for Elizabethan stages both public or in banqueting rooms (*Early English Stages*, II, Pt. 1, p. 267).

From square, circular or hexagonal theatre walls tiered with galleries for spectators, the Elizabethan stage jutted out over six feet above ground level and occupied about half the floor space where the spectators could stand on three sides of it. The stage of the Fortune theatre was 43 feet × 27 feet and the floor area in which it stood was 55 feet × 55 feet. At the back of the stage the lowest tier of spectators' galleries gave place to a curtained recess or inner stage, a study or discovery space, used for interior scenes. Another view is that there was no recess, but a curtained space under a canopy in front of the rear wall of the stage. On either side were dressing rooms from which entrance doors opened on to the stage. The first floor gallery behind the stage was used for scenes in the play; a second floor gallery or room was used by musicians. Above the balcony and covering the rear portion of the stage was a canopy or roof painted blue and adorned with stars sometimes supported by pillars from the stage. There were trap-doors in the stage and frequently a low rail around it.

The pillars, canopy, railings and back stage were painted and adorned. If a tragedy was to be performed, the stage was hung with black, but there was no stage setting in the modern fashion.

It has recently been argued very strongly by I. A. Shapiro (*Shakespeare Studies*, 2, Cincinnati, 1966, pp. 192–209) that the woodcut

Courtesy of the British Council

MODEL OF AN ELIZABETHAN THEATRE
by Richard Southern

of the memory theatre in Fludd's *Ars Memoriae*, which F. Yates suggested in her *Art of Memory* was a representation of the second Globe theatre, is rather a representation of the private Blackfriars theatre where *Antony and Cleopatra* was at one time produced. Yates expanded her views in *Theatre of the World*, 1969. It will be noticed that there is a chamber projecting from the middle of the balcony backstage, the balcony having entrances at both ends. Such a construction would greatly facilitate the raising of Antony into the monument (*Antony and Cleopatra*, IV. xv).

There were stage properties usually of the kind that could be easily pushed on and off the stage. Records of the time mention a mossy bank a wall, a bed, trees, arbours, thrones, tents, rock, tomb, hell-mouth, a cauldron; on the other hand tents, pavilions and mansions may have been permanent 'sets' in some historical plays. These structures varied in size for a small one may have sufficed for the tomb in *Romeo and Juliet*, but the tent representing the Queen's chamber in Peele's *Edward I* contained six adults and a bed, as Armstrong pointed out. On the whole properties were limited to essentials although the popularity of the private masques with their painted canvas sets encouraged increasing elaboration of scenery and spectacle during the reign of James I.

There was no limitation to the display of rich and gorgeous costumes in the current fashion of the day. The more magnificent and splendid the better; indeed the costumes must have been the most expensive item in the requirements of the company. An occasional attempt was made at period costume, but normally plays were produced in Elizabethan garments without any suspicion of the oddness that strikes us when we read of Cæsar entering 'in his nightshirt' or Cleopatra calling on Charmian to cut the lace of what we may call her corsets. High rank was marked by magnificence of dress, a trade or calling by functional clothes. Feste, the clown, would wear the traditional fool's coat or petticoat of motley, a corase cloth of mixed yellow and green. The coat was buttoned from the neck to the girdle from which hung a wooden dagger, its skirts voluminous with capacious pockets in which Feste might 'impetticoat' any 'gratillity'. Ghosts, who appear in a number of plays, wore a kind of leathern smock. Oberon and magicians such as Prospero wore, in the delightful phrase and spelling of the records, 'a robe for to goo invisibell'.

The actors formed companies under the patronage of noblemen for

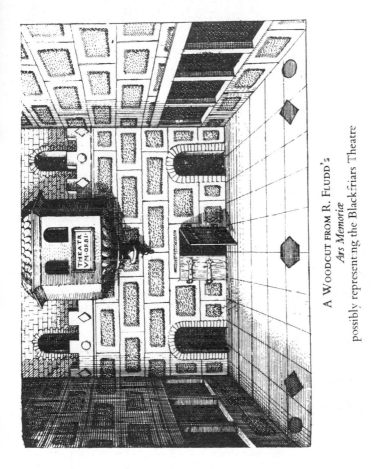

A WOODCUT FROM R. FLUDD'S
Ars Memoriæ
possibly representing the Blackfriars Theatre

protection against a civic law condemning them as 'rogues, vagabonds and sturdy beggars' to severe punishment. They were the servants of their patron and wore his livery. The company was a co-operative society, its members jointly owned the property and shared the profits; thus Shakespeare's plays were not his to use as he liked, they belonged to his company, the Lord Chamberlain's Men. This company, honoured by James I when it became the King's Men, was the most successful company of the period. It had a number of distinguished actors, it achieved more Court performances than any other company, and it performed in the best London theatre, the Globe, until it was burnt down during a performance of *Henry VIII* in 1613. Women were not allowed on the public stage, although they performed in masques and theatricals in private houses. Boys, therefore, were apprenticed to the leading actors and took the female parts.

An almost unbelievable number of plays was produced by the companies. It has been shown for example that in a fortnight eleven performances of ten different plays were presented by one company at one theatre. The companies were in effect repertory companies. Their productions consisted of new plays, and old plays either repeated without change, or revised sometimes extensively. It is to be wondered how far the actors achieved word-perfection in their parts. Their versatility and their team work no doubt helped to overcome the burden of such rapid changes of parts. Indeed although the main parts in a play were performed by a small select group of actors, there is little evidence of type-casting apart from the clowns, or that plays were written with particular actors in mind.

The audience in the public theatres was drawn from all classes. There were courtiers and inns of court men who appreciated intricate word play, mythological allusions and the technique of sword play; there were the 'groundlings' who liked jigs, horse-play and flamboyance of speech and spectacle; and there were the citizens who appreciated the romantic stories, the high eloquence of patriotic plays and moral sentiments. A successful play would have something for all. Sometimes gallants would sit on a stool on the stage and behave rather like the courtiers in V. i, or *Love's Labour's Lost*, V. ii. The 'groundlings' too were likely to be troublesome and noisy. They could buy bottled-beer, oranges and nuts for their comfort; but it is noted to their credit that when Falstaff appeared on the stage, so popular was he that they stopped cracking nuts! They applauded a well delivered speech; they hissed a boring play; they even rioted and severely damaged one theatre. Shakespeare's plays however were popular among all classes: at Court they

did so take Eliza and our James,

and elsewhere in the public theatre they outshone the plays of other dramatists. Any play of his was assured of a 'full house'. An ardent theatre-goer of the day praising Shakespeare's plays above those of other dramatists wrote:

When let but Falstaff come,
Hal, Poins, the rest, you scarce shall have a room,
All is so pester'd; let but Beatrice
And Benedick be seen, lo in a trice
The cockpit, galleries, boxes, all are full
To hear Malvolio, that cross-garter'd gull.

Shakespeare's Works

The year of composition of only a few of Shakespeare's plays can be determined with certainty. The following list is based on current scholarly opinion.

The plays marked with an asterisk were not included in the First Folio edition of Shakespeare's plays (1623) which was prepared by Heminge and Condell, Shakespeare's fellow actors. Shakespeare's part in them has been much debated.

1590–1   2 Henry VI, 3 Henry VI.
1591–2   1 Henry VI.
1592–3   Richard III, Comedy of Errors.
1593–4   Titus Andronicus, Taming of the Shrew, Sir Thomas More* (Part authorship. Four manuscript pages presumed to be in Shakespeare's hand).
1594–5   Two Gentlemen of Verona, Love's Labour's Lost, Romeo and Juliet, Edward III* (Part authorship).
1595–6   Richard II, A Midsummer Night's Dream.
1596–7   King John, Merchant of Venice, Love's Labour Won (Not extant. Before 1598).
1597–8   1 Henry IV, 2 Henry IV, The Merry Wives of Windsor.
1598–9   Much Ado About Nothing, Henry V.
1599–1600   Julius Caesar, As You Like It.
1600–1   Hamlet, Twelfth Night.
1601–2   Troilus and Cressida.
1602–3   All's Well that Ends Well.